CW01095948

With the Madras Regiment in Burma

With the Madras European Regiment in Burma

The Experiences of an Officer of the
Honourable East India Company's Army
During the First Anglo-Burmese War
1824 - 1826

John Butler

with

A Brief History of the Army of the
Honourable East India Company

by G. F. MacMunn

LEONAUR

With the Madras European Regiment in Burma: the Experiences of an Officer of the Honourable East India Company's Army During the First Anglo-Burmese War 1824 - 1826
by John Butler

with:
A Brief History of the Army of the Honourable East India Company
by G. F. MacMunn

Originally published under the title
A Sketch of the Services of the Madras European Regiment During the Burmese War.

A Brief History of the Army of the Honourable East India Company
is adapted from the 1911 volume:
The Armies Of India
by A. C. Lovett & G. F. MacMunn

Published by Leonaur Ltd

Copyright in this form © 2007 Leonaur Ltd

ISBN (10 digit): 1-84677-146-3 (hardcover)
ISBN (13 digit): 978-1-84677-146-0 (hardcover)

ISBN (10 digit): 1-84677-138-2 (softcover)
ISBN (13 digit): 978-1-84677-138-5 (softcover)

http://www.leonaur.com

Publisher's Notes

In the interests of authenticity, the spellings, grammar and place names used have been retained from the original editions.

The opinions of the authors represent a view of events in which he was a participant related from his own perspective, as such the text is relevant as an historical document.

The views expressed in this book are not necessarily those of the publisher.

Contents

Preface

The following pages are only intended for the perusal of those who are immediately connected with the Regiment, and who will feel a particular interest in the record of its recent services during the war in Burmah.

I may be allowed to preface my slight narrative with a few words on the past history of the corps to which I have the honour to belong. Though it cannot boast an antiquity like that of Her Majesty's 1st, or Royal Regiment, which is said to have been Julius Caesar's bodyguard, the Madras European Regiment can refer to a date coeval with the first great achievements of the British arms in India. The corps was in existence prior to the year 1746, when the town of Madras was besieged by the French. At that critical era, when the Carnatic was so incessantly engaged in warfare, the Regiment took an active and distinguished part under those renowned Commanders, Lawrence and Clive, and was present at most of the engagements which took place between the French and English, up to the year 1756, when it embarked with Colonel Clive for the recovery of Calcutta, and was present at the celebrated battle of Plassey in June, 1757.

During the turbulent period which so long oppressed the eastern coast of Coromandel, the Regiment was present with Colonel Ford at the capture of Masulipatam in 1759;

likewise at the battle of Wandewaish in 1760, under the command of Colonel Coote; afterwards at the capture of Arcot, and the siege and capture of Pondicherry. The Madras European Regiment was constantly employed against those formidable opponents to British ascendancy in India; Hyder Ally, and his son Tippoo Sultan, until the fall of Seringapatam in 1799—an event which for a time restored tranquillity to the peninsula of India.

The services of the Regiment, were, however, again called for when an expedition was sent to the Eastward, in 1809, and it was present at the capture of Amboyna, Bada, Ternate, etc. The late Major General Sir John Malcolm, G.C.B., distinguished in British Indian Annals no less by his services as a statesman than as a soldier, commenced his military career as an Ensign in this Regiment, and he had the gratification of witnessing once more the gallantry of his own corps during the whole of the Mahratta campaign in 1817, and 1818, on which occasion the regiment was actively employed, and shared the honours reaped at the battles of Mahidpoor, Mulligawn, Talnair, and Asseerghur.

The following brief memoir of the services of the Regiment during the Burmese war, will speak for itself; and, I trust that, from a perusal of it, the Regiment will be considered as still upholding that reputation for gallantry which has ever distinguished it in former periods. Though upwards of thirteen years have elapsed since the termination of the Ava war, and though the services of the Madras European Regiment during that eventful time were intimately connected with many of its most stirring scenes, no attempt has yet been made to narrate them. The impressions which they have left, though vivid, have not been recorded by any one; and though I make no pretensions to any other merit of authorship, than mere fidelity, I cannot but think that an attempt to note down those impressions, and to preserve some of those pleasing and proud recollections, will be acceptable, not only to my brother officers who themselves bore a part in those scenes, but to those who, equally sharing their zeal and pride in the Regiment, were, nevertheless, not so fortunate as to participate personally in its dangers and its triumphs during this memorable period.

I claim the indulgence of all alike, for the imperfections of my attempt to do justice to a subject worthier of a more eloquent pen. To those who were, like myself, actors in those scenes, I have to return my best thanks for the reminiscences and descriptions they have given me, of many occurrences of the time which did not happen to fall immediately under my own personal observation. These details have enabled me to fill up the outline of my little narrative much more fully than I could otherwise have done.

CHAPTER 1
Setting Sail for Burmah

How well do I remember the day on which we received intelligence that the regiment was to be employed in active service, by a letter from Sir Alexander Campbell, the Commander-in-Chief, to our commanding officer, Lieutenant-Colonel H. Kelly, desiring him to hold his Corps in readiness for embarkation, to form part of an expedition then fitting out against the Burmese Empire.

The regiment was all in commotion, and every one sought for information as to this new scene of operations; of which, however, there was but little to be obtained, as, with the exception of Colonel Symes's imperfect history, written many years previously, nothing was known of the people or country we were soon to invade. Nothing could exceed the joy expressed by all parties at the prospect of being actively employed on service; and none but those who have long experienced the irksome monotony attending a garrison life in India, could fully appreciate the out-burst of feeling and delight expressed throughout the corps on the receipt of this intelligence: the excitement of expectation amounted almost to enthusiasm.

The mess-table on that day was a scene of uproarious mirth; and a number of quiet inexperienced young officers, who had but lately joined the regiment, came in for an unmerciful share of banter from the old hands, who prophesied that such delicate young gentlemen would soon be sent to the hospital, and that a few marches would do for them. Nevertheless they proved themselves, on trial, well capable of sustaining the credit of the regiment for gallantry and patient endurance of the hardships of active warfare; indeed, I am inclined to think your quiet and gentle characters have often most real firmness.

On this expedition officers were permitted to take only a limited quantity of baggage; the number of servants was also limited according to the rank of the officers. Horses were quite out of the question, except for the staff; and government supplied each officer with a small Gorka tent six feet square, for which act of grace we had to pay far more than we were generally obliged to give for the large and comfortable tents which we were now compelled to leave behind, and which, for want of carriage, indeed, would have been useless to us in Burmah.

A subaltern, even in India, is seldom troubled with a superfluous kit; and on this occasion a judicious selection of the most serviceable articles absolutely necessary, was soon completed. Like most young soldiers, we were highly impatient for the arrival of the transports to convey us to the wished-for scene of action, and I do not suppose the fort of Masulipatam had ever been the scene of such stirring hubbub as on the present occasion. The ramparts were daily thronged with lookers-out for the vessels which were to convey us across the bay, and now and then one of the most expert in climbing would be seen, sitting on the cap of the flag-staff, that he might have the pleasure of giving the first joyful intelligence of the ships being in sight.

However, it was not until the 11th of April 1824, about five o'clock in the afternoon, that they were espied coming into the roads with a strong sea-breeze, which soon brought them to an anchor. If there was any stir amongst us before this, the arrival of the vessels increased it twofold. Not a soldier remained in the barracks: the whole regiment rushed to the ramparts with a degree of interest and excitement I have seldom witnessed.

The commanders landed shortly after eight o'clock, to report their arrival to the officer commanding the garrison; and working parties were immediately ordered to convey the ammunition for the regiment, to the boats lying off the wharf in readiness to take it on board; which was not completed till past eleven o'clock at night; when the commotions of the day subsided, and once more all was quiet.

The wild and fanciful visions of a young soldier first going on the service, are not to be described, if his imagination is full of events that are never likely to happen; and though his anticipations of honour and distinction are seldom realised, his short-lived dream is one of exquisite pleasure, and is never forgotten. The cherished hopes and anticipations of our early years, although never fulfilled, are treasured as the remembrance of a dear but departed friend whom we shall see no more.

As soon as the gun fired, the next morning, all hands were on the move, and two companies were soon under arms and on their way to the jetty, with the drum and fife at their head, playing "The British Grenadiers." From the nature of the expedition, no women were allowed to follow the regiment as is usually the custom; and it was a distressing scene to witness the wives and children of the men, following the boats down the river as far as they could, crying and sobbing as though their hearts would break. Many of these poor women waded into the sea, following the boats, until their voices could be no longer heard. It was their last farewell with most of them—for of the eight hundred and sixty-three brave men who embarked on this occasion, not more than one hundred returned at the expiration of the war in 1826. The remainder are at rest.

CHAPTER 2

The Andaman Isle

From the distance at which the shipping were obliged to lie off shore at Masulipatam, in consequence of the shallowness of water, it took two days before the regiment embarked, and we did not weigh anchor until the evening of the 13th, when we took our last farewell look of land, and were left to reflect on the glorious uncertainty of war. Nothing of interest occurred from the day of our embarkation on board the transports, *Bannerman, David Clarke* and *George IV* until our arrival at Port Cornwallis in the isle of Andaman, on the eastern side of the bay of Bengal; where we were joined by a fleet of ships and gunboats, the former having on board H. M.'s 13th and 38th regiments from Calcutta.

The harbour of Port Cornwallis is spacious and secure, and is surrounded by large and lofty trees down to the water's edge and so dense is the jungle as to be nearly impenetrable. Shellfish and oysters abound among the rocks, and constitute the principal food of the few natives inhabiting the island. It was mentioned that a boat going on shore with some of H. M.'s 13th before we arrived, had been fired on by the inhabitants, with bows and arrows; but we saw none of them, with the exception of a dead body lying on the shore. The body was that of a female, and quite naked; her skin was of a jet black colour, the lips thick, with a flat nose and woolly hair, and when alive must have been a most unlovable object, although apparently in the prime of life.

This island was selected by the British Indian government as a convict station in 1791, but was abandoned in consequence of the unhealthiness of the climate, and some disputes with the savage inhabitants. The harbour swarms with sharks, one of was shot by an officer of the regiment, and in an instant after, upwards of a dozen of these monsters, attracted by the blood, fought desperately for a share of the prize, which they devoured in a few seconds. In less than ten minutes afterwards, a private of the regiment, named Gallagher, jumped overboard and swam round the ship without the slightest fear, and came on board again by a rope thrown to him by some of the sailors: I need not say that he was punished for his hardihood and folly.

The fleet remained two days at this port to take in a supply of water, which is here very pure: the harbour is one of the most secure places for shipping to assemble at, from its being landlocked on every side, and safe from sudden squalls, as well as from its also being very deep. On the 7th May, about one o'clock, the Commodore fired a gun and hoisted the signal for all vessels to weigh anchor and put to sea and it was an exceedingly animated and beautiful sight, as ship after ship spread her sails to the wind, and steered for the entrance of the harbour, which is one of the most beautiful that can be imagined. A six knot breeze soon carried them into blue water, and without an accident, although the *Bannerman* very nearly ran down a pretty little schooner laden with powder, and it was by the greatest chance she escaped.

Rather a stiff gale came on the night of our quitting Port Cornwallis, and the next morning our fleet was scattered all over the horizon; the transport *Hastings* was nearly hull down to leeward of all the others, and was in so pitiable a condition that His Majesty's brig *Sophie* was sent to take her in tow. The morning of the 10th of May saw us at anchor in little more than five fathoms water (which was very muddy,) at the entrance of the Rangoon river, a branch of the Irrawaddy. This, however, was not accomplished without some confusion and damage amongst the shipping.

As the *George IV*, with part of the regiment on board, was about to anchor, the greater part of her sail having been taken in, she was unable to make head against the strong current, which runs here at the rate of twelve knots an hour, and she made stern-way so rapidly that before the evil could be remedied, she drove down on the *Earl Kelly*, then swung round and struck her bows against the *Virginia* and got completely entangled with that vessel. I can give but a faint description of the confusion and uproar which followed: fore and main-top-masts, gib, boom, and I don't know what else, came down, and the ship heeled over so much, laying broad side to the current between the two ships, that it was with difficulty we could keep our feet. She was, however, released from this critical situation by the captain of the *Earl Kelly* slipping his cable, which separated the ships, and allowed the *George*

IV to float quietly down to a more secure anchorage, her captain receiving the hearty maledictions of every skipper whose ship he passed, for his want of seamanship; which he bore very quietly; and when hailed by the captain of the *Bannerman*, said it was "all in the way of business".

It was a scene of the utmost confusion; the deck was crowded with soldiers, and yards and blocks were falling about them on every side; orders and imprecations came together and from all quarters, and produced a scene of uproar and commotion which it is difficult to describe.

Sam Gover, our little skipper, was a generous fellow, and treated us most liberally throughout the voyage; but whether he is now dead, or still in the land of the living, I know not—I fear that he has long since fallen a victim to an ardent and enthusiastic love of alcohol. The commanders of transports did not at all like considering themselves under the orders of naval officers, and submitting to discipline.

On the passage to Rangoon our little skipper deviated from his course, and attempted to get away from the fleet, but was soon brought back by a well directed shot that convinced him he was by no means out of reach. During our stay at Port Cornwallis, he refused to obey the orders of the Commodore to discontinue sending his boats for water; and when ordered to repair on board the Commodore's ship, flatly refused, saying, that he had nothing to do with him. However, the appearance of a lieutenant with a party of marines on his quarter-deck, who took the little man into custody, soon brought him to his senses. It bore a little too much the semblance of reality on the Commodore's part, to be resisted.

CHAPTER 3

Rangoon

Rangoon is situated on the north bank of the eastern branch of the Irrawaddy river, at the distance of about thirty miles from the entrance where, as I have stated, the fleet came to an anchor on the 10th of May. During that night many beacon-fires were seen on the banks of the river, evidently for the purpose of communicating the intelligence of the approach of an enemy; and it appeared, as we afterwards heard, that this was the first information the inhabitants of Rangoon received of a hostile force being so unpleasantly near to them.

The next morning the fleet again weighed anchor, the Commodore leading the van in H. M's frigate the *Liffy* of fifty-six guns; and Captain Crisp, of the *Bannerman*, who had traded for some years to Rangoon was ordered on board to pilot her up safely, as the navigation of the river is dangerous, and requires a person well acquainted with the shoals and sand-banks to prevent a vessel from grounding. All the ships followed the Commodore in succession, keeping a respectful distance from each other to prevent accidents; a wise precaution, for a heavy black squall came on, which for some minutes enveloped the whole fleet in darkness, driving us on at the rate of nine or ten knots an hour. This squall suddenly cleared up, the dark clouds quickly vanished, and the Great Shoe Dagon Pagoda, or Golden Temple of Rangoon, stood disclosed to our view.

The scene, so unexpectedly discovered, was magnificent in the extreme; the sun shone full on the temple, which had been cleansed by the rain, and it glittered most resplendently. This elegant structure towered majestically above the lofty trees which surrounded it; and their dark green leaves, bespangled by the rain and sparkling in the sun's rays, contributed not a little to the brilliant effect of the scene. It was now that our expectations were raised as to the prize-money that must be in store for us in so wealthy a country as this appeared to be; and many surmises passed in our minds, as to the *lute* we should have on landing.

We found H. M's sloop of war, the *Lame*, hard and fast on a sand-bank, where she remained until the tide ebbed, which enabled her indefatigable and enterprising commander (Captain Marriott) to warp her off into the proper channel. A few straggling shots were fired from the banks of the river as the shipping passed up, but it was harmless, and was not returned by us.

Had the fleet gone up to Rangoon on the 10th, instead of waiting four-and-twenty hours at the mouth of the river, it is more than probable we should have secured the greater part of the inhabitants; but in consequence of our delay, the whole town was stripped, and not a vestige of anything was found by the troops on landing.

It was not the intention of the General to fire on the town, or be the aggressor, as it was of the utmost importance to the force that the inhabitants should remain peaceably and quietly in their houses. But a small battery on the principal wharf opened a fire on the *Liffy*, which was a signal for the commencement of hostilities; a broadside or two, which killed several of their gunners, soon put an end to the firing.

The quarter-master-general of the forces was now busily employed in communicating the General's orders for disembarking such part of the force as was requisite to take possession of the town. His duty was soon performed, and the landing effected at the principal wharf, as the place was found vacated.

While a party of reconnaissance was passing the arsenal, situated in the principal street of the town, they found three European merchants tied to posts for the purpose of being executed, by order of the Kee Woongee, or governor of Rangoon. The evidence given by them when released and taken before Sir A. Campbell, was, that the Kee Woongee had ordered them to be executed in consequence of their being Englishmen; as he said they must have been well aware that an English force was about to invade the country, and that he considered them in the light of spies. He ordered them accordingly to be tied up with their hands behind them, ready for execution, and the headsman was actually parading up and down in front of these unfortunate men, and going through the mockery of sharpening his sword that he might execute his office neatly, when the fleet arrived.

Luckily for these poor fellows, the Kee Wongee was busily engaged in giving some orders which delayed the final mandate for their execution; and while standing at the entrance of the arsenal, the *Liffy's* fire opened with such good effect that he had only time to think of his own safety. He and his people fled, leaving their intended victims in the state which I have described.

At the time the reconnaissance party found these poor fellows, they were half dead from apprehension: knowing full well the cruelty of the Burmese character, they were aware that no mercy could be expected at their hands. The arsenal bore evident marks of the *Liffy's* fire having been well directed; it must have been rather too warm to be pleasant, for we saw shot-holes in the wall that admitted daylight, so that the prisoners ran a two-fold risk of their lives. The officers of the party who released these merchants, said it was quite affecting to witness the tears of joy shed by them on their release, and still more so from the venerable appearance of one of them, who was upwards of sixty years old, his hair silvered with age.

On the same day that the town of Rangoon was captured, two companies of the regiment disembarked on the opposite side of the river at the town of Dallah, which we took possession of without resistance. These two companies were landed for the double purpose of preventing the enemy from assembling in that quarter, as well as for the protection of H. M. S. *Lame*, which had grounded on a sandbank just opposite the town. The necessary precaution of posting guards and sentries being soon taken, we established ourselves for the night in the vacant houses of our now absent friends the Burmese, who had evidently quitted in much hurry and confusion, as we found their cooking utensils on the fires, which were still alight.

It was about the middle of the night, as near as I can recollect, when I was aroused from my sleep by the orderly serjeant of my company, who reported that some of the men mere absent, and that others appeared to have been drinking, and he was confident there must be an arrack-shop somewhere in the neighbourhood. Of course I instantly started to my feet, and went in search of the absentees, who were found in the house of a Chinaman not far off, regaling most joyously. On such an occasion the appearance of an officer was sufficient to put the whole party to flight, and every man took to his heels as if the devil was after him, clearing everything that came in their way until they got out of the house. I wanted to secure some of the offenders, and followed one man pretty closely till he came to a wall; and now it was Hobson's choice with him, neck or nothing; but he was hard pressed, and cleared it in sty... however, he was little aware of what was on the oth... ...into a pond, which, luckily ...do him any injury, but ...there I left him to qua... ...g.

On my retu... ...oached some twenty o... ...r security lodged the ...for the remainder of t... ...st well pleased with th... ...ien the troops landed ...id that it was deserted by the inhabitants, they wandered about in all directions to see what could be found; when, by some chance, a large party of Europeans discovered a cellar adjoining the house of one of the merchants, where there was a considerable quantity of brandy, which was soon broached, and the men as soon drunk. Information of this discovery quickly spread amongst the other part of the troops, who soon followed their example, and by night-time the greater part of the European force in the town were intoxicated, and in this state they went rambling about from house to house with lighted torches, and as may be fully anticipated, the town was set on fire and a great portion of it consumed in consequence. Some of the officers, who had found out where the men had been drinking, repaired to the house and destroyed all the spirits they could find, by letting it flow on the ground but the damage was done.

Fortunately for the troops in Rangoon, there was not a watchful enemy near them, as, from the state they were then in, few could have offered much resistance, had an attempt been made to retake the town. From the houses in Burmah being built of wood and bamboos, the flames spread rapidly. The night was intensely dark, and the conflagration was certainly a magnificent sight, seen from the opposite side of the river at Dallah, where the regiment was stationed. Boats from the different ships were quickly manned, and the praiseworthy and fearless exertions of the sailors soon managed to check and eventually extinguish the fire, but not before nearly half the town had been consumed.

On the morning of the 12th, the remainder of the troops were disembarked for the purpose of taking up lines which had been portioned out by the quarter-master-general of the forces, and the companies of our regiment on the Dallah side crossed over likewise. Many of the men cut a curious and ludicrous appearance when we assembled at the wharf on landing, as most of them had managed, to *lute* something; many were laden with ducks and fowls purloined from the houses where we had taken up our abode the night before, and others had silks, China mats, and a variety of other articles.

Just before the Colonel of the regiment was going to move us off, the General who happened to be passing by at the time, observed some of these appendages attached to the pouches of the men, where they had slung them for security, and, as they imagined, out of the way of observation; but the ducks betrayed them, for they gave such audible evidence of their presence, that the General could not avoid seeing them, and he sent his aid-de-camp to the Colonel directing him to order the release of the feathered tribe immediately, and to say that he was astonished at observing so great a laxity of discipline on the part of the officers. The ducks were accordingly let loose; but when we moved onwards, and the General was out of sight, they were again secured; and effectually to prevent a second betrayal, their necks were wrung.

We marched about a mile from the town on a fine broad road leading up to the Pagoda, and took up our quarters in some good substantial houses on the left of the road, between H. M.'s 41st regiment and 9th regiment N.I. The houses are all built upon piles from four to fourteen feet from the ground, and are entered by ladders for that purpose. In our lines there were several Poongee houses, the best in the place, the residence of their priests: these houses are all built of wood, and furnished excellent accommodation for the men and officers. Two regiments were stationed in the stockade at Rangoon, and H. M.'s 13th and 38th regiments occupied lines round the base of the great Pagoda; while the road leading from the stockade to the Pagoda, was occupied, as I have already mentioned, by H. M.'s 41st, the Madras, European regiment, and the 9th regiment N.I., each regiment throwing out pickets and sentries in its immediate front, and connected with those of the regiments on either side of them, thus forming a secure chain of posts for more than two miles from the stockade to the Pagoda.

It must not be supposed, although we had taken up our lines, that we were permitted by the Burmese to remain quiet possessors of their houses; and from the nature of the vicinity of Rangoon they had ample means afforded them of annoying our pickets, and causing at times a good deal of firing, for the grass was high, and the jungle close around us, and in some parts very thick. Our outline picket was, I think, one of the worst situated of any, as the grass was so high in some parts as almost to conceal the sentries from each other, and in some spots we were obliged to raise mounds of earth that the sentries might see about them and at the same time be more secure from surprise; for the Burmese used to creep up on their hands and knees so silently through the long grass, as to approach within a few paces of a sentry without being perceived, when they would dart their spears at him, and glide away as swiftly as possible.

Our pickets and sentries were kept constantly on the alert by secret and daring attacks of this nature, as they were unable to discover what force might be coming against them at night, when the enemy were lurking about the different pickets: this was often the cause of a good deal of firing. Indeed, I must confess that the men were not so steady at first as they became in a very short time after; but there was every excuse for young soldiers, placed in a position where they could not see ten paces before them, in the midst of high grass, and surrounded by such an active and daring enemy.

The town of Rangoon is stockaded, and stands on the north bank of the river at the distance of about thirty miles from the sea, and is said to be three miles in circumference. The stockade is formed of solid teak-wood piles fifteen feet high, joined at the top by beams transversely placed, with embrasures at every four feet. It has four gateways, or entrances, corresponding with the four principal streets, which are narrow, but straight and good.

Two miles from Rangoon stands the beautiful Shoe Dagon Pagoda, surrounded by innumerable images of Guadama. It is situated on a hill, and is approached by a long flight of steps, and the terrace is said to be nine hundred feet in length, and nearly seven hundred broad. One of the finest prospects in the vicinity of Rangoon is from this pagoda. In front, and as far as the eye can reach, you see a dense, but beautifully wooded country. On the right, at the foot of the hill, are several large sheets of water, and innumerable pagodas; and beyond this the Pegue river is seen winding through an extensive plain of rich meadows towards the hills of Syriam, where it disappears within a forest of trees. Behind, lies the stockade of Rangoon, with the town of Dallah just peeping out between the masts of the shipping in the river, and the spires of innumerable pagodas in all parts of the lines. But I am no hand at description, and must leave the imagination to complete the picture.

CHAPTER 4

Into the Jungle

Our first excursion into the country was on the 14th of May, two days subsequent to the landing of the force. At an early hour on that morning, a party of reconnaissance, of which the flank companies of the regiment formed part, under the command of Lieutenant-Colonel Hodgson, was formed upon the high road leading to the pagoda. The sun had risen some time before we commenced our march, and after a toilsome journey of three hours we halted at a small village, from which the natives made a rapid retreat when they caught sight of us.

The object of this journey was to distribute proclamations calling on the inhabitants of Rangoon to return to their houses; and our hopes of success rested on being able to hold a parlance with some of the natives. But nothing would induce them to meet us; which Colonel Hodgson attributed to their distrust of our motives, and consequently determined, by a bold measure, to secure their confidence. Accompanied only by a Burmese interpreter, with a green branch of a tree in his hand, as a token of peace, he walked leisurely across the plain at the foot of the village, and entered the jungle where we had seen the natives assemble after our arrival.

For more than half an hour we neither saw or heard any thing of him; in fact, we began to have serious apprehensions for his safety, and were on the point of sending out a party to look for him, when he made his appearance in company with three or four Burmese, one of them carrying his sword.

As they approached our party they appeared uneasy, and suspicious, and squatted themselves down at some distance from us, we did not let them see that we observed their mistrust of us; but offered them cigars and some biscuit, and in a short time they became somewhat more sociable. We could not, however, prevail on any of them to return to Rangoon with us, as they said their families would be killed if they were to do so. I have seldom witnessed more cool courage than was displayed by Colonel Hodgson on this occasion. He instantly divined the feelings of the Burmese, and acted on that knowledge with equal fortitude and coolness; it was just one of those acts of calm moral courage that stamp the character of a man forever, as a fearless soldier.

As this was our first march after a month's confinement on board ship, we were all a good deal fagged, and heartily glad when we got back to camp. Here we remained for some days, agreeably occupied in catching Burmese bullocks; and I am sure that I am far within the mark, when I say, that at least four thousand head of cattle were at this time to be found within our lines. An order from Sir A. Campbell, however, compelled us to liberate all that we had laid our hands on, and in a few days they escaped into the jungle.

It appears strange, after such an act of forbearance, that Sir A. Campbell should not have extended his protection to public as well as private property; that he did not, was evident by the attack he shortly after made on the bowels of the Great Pagoda, which was continued with the utmost perseverance until every hope of finding the long expected treasure vanished; but it was not long before the effects of this example showed itself in the conduct of the troops; they doubtless thought it a precedent worthy of imitation; and as the General confined his operations to the Great Pagoda, the soldiers commenced work on the smaller, and in a short time there was scarcely a pagoda that was not rifled.

These pagodas contained numerous small gold and silver images, of no great value except as curiosities; though I knew an officer who laid out three hundred rupees in the purchase of a great number of them, obtained in one night, by a single company that happened to be stationed near a small square of the pagodas. They were sent to Calcutta on speculation, and I believe the officer made a good deal by them.

Our next excursion was under General MacBean, who at this time commanded the Madras division of the army. We started at an early hour, leaving the Great Pagoda on our left. We passed the Scotch tank, so named from its possessing peculiar medicinal qualities, and plunged into the jungle. This day I was with the rear of the column, and we were kept at a long trot the whole march—which is generally the case with the rear, where the road is rough, and the troops are not made to close up; for as soon as the head of the column comes to a piece of bad ground, they open out to select the best part of the road to pass over, and this delays the rear who are afterwards obliged to regain their position at the double, After a march of three or four hours, as the head of the column got clear of the jungle, they came suddenly upon an armed party of Burmese, drawn up in front of a village, apparently determined to offer resistance; but as our force advanced, they fired and ran off.

Although the rear of the column increased its pace as soon as the firing was heard, we were too late to see anything of the enemy; they had disappeared in the surrounding jungle, and as the General concluded that we should see nothing more of them, we were ordered to take up our quarters in the village, which was found to be deserted. After the necessary precautions of posting guards and sentries, we piled arms, and broke off to refresh ourselves before returning to camp. Had we gone a mile farther we should have fallen in with two large stockades at Joazong, occupied in force by the Burmese, but of this we knew nothing till some days later, when H. M.'s 13th and 38th regiments had the good fortune to fall in with them, as I shall presently relate.

I took up my quarters in a large house, and I believe it was one of the best in the village; but I was not a little surprised to find it occupied by a very good looking young woman, who was rocking a child to sleep as quietly and unconcernedly as if she had been in the midst of her own friends; neither did she show the least symptom of fear or disquiet when a brother officer and myself entered her house. Shortly after, several of the officers made their appearance, and we agreed to club the contents of our haversacks, which by-the-bye contained nothing but mouldy biscuit and salt beef: however, we wound up with that best of Indian luxuries, a cheroot, in which the young Burmese lady joined us very cordially. During our short stay at this village, some of our men brought in a Burmese, whose leg was broken below the knee, apparently by a musket-ball.

I heard that he was afterwards taken into Rangoon, and that his leg was amputated, which he submitted to with great coolness; and when the operation was completed, held out the other leg, and appeared surprised when the surgeon declined taking that off also. Surgery appears to be unknown to the Burmese, and in all cases of wounds they merely wash and tie up the injured part with leaves, and trust to time and nature for the cure.

The sound of the assembly soon recalled the stragglers, and in less than a quarter of an hour, the party were again under arms, and on their way back to camp. Grazing in the fields by the wayside, we saw some buffaloes of an enormous size, and I think nothing short of military discipline could have prevented us from converting them into steaks to satisfy the cravings of our hungry stomachs, for it must be borne in mind that salt rations and weevil biscuit had been our daily fare since we landed, with the exception of pineapples, which abounded in the gardens round Rangoon; and from an over-indulgence of this delicious fruit, I have no doubt our men suffered severely.

I have already stated that it was the good fortune of

H. M.'s 13th and 38th regiments to fall in with two of the enemy's stockades at Joazong a few days later, about a mile in advance of the village I have been speaking of; but as no part of our regiment was employed on this expedition, which was led by Sir A. Campbell in person, it is unnecessary for me to say more than that the Burmese made a most determined resistance, and it was said that upwards of three hundred of them were killed in the stockades; the loss on our side was also great, including two officers killed, and one so severely wounded, that he was obliged to have his leg amputated.

CHAPTER 5

Storming the Half-Way Stockade

On the following morning, the 29th of May, the flank companies of the regiment formed part of a force under the command of General MacBean, and proceeded in the direction of the stockades at Joazong, captured by Sir A. Campbell the day before, in expectation of finding other works farther in advance. The plains were covered with water, from the rains which had now set in heavily, and as we had to wade through paddy-fields above our knees in mud and water for a considerable distance, we were more than usually fatigued, although our march was by no means a long one, our progress being stopped by the river Moriee, which we were unable to cross for want of boats.

While resting ourselves on the bank of this river, an officer told me that he had fallen in with a soldier of the regiment in rear of the column, who complained of being very unwell, and that he had given him a good stiff screw of brandy to help him on; but we never saw the poor fellow again, and it was not till the end of the war that we learnt that he had been taken prisoner by the Burmese, and sent up to the court of Ava. On our way back to camp, I gladly availed myself of the opportunity to visit the Joazong stockades, and it was truly a pitiable sight; for the dead were numerous, and in all stages of corruption. Byron has said with great truth—

When all is past, it is humbling to tread,
O'er the weltering field of the tombless dead,
And see the worms of the earth, and fowls of the air,
Beast of the forest, all gathering there,
All regarding man as their prey,
All rejoicing in his decay.

One day about this time, Corporal Lucas of the regiment, told me that he had caught a very nice pony in the jungle just below the picket, and that I was welcome to the animal if I would send for him. Although I found the poor beast nearly starved, still I thought myself a very lucky fellow, and anticipated many a ride when my brother officers mould be obliged to walk; unfortunately, the following day we made a long march into the country, when I was prevailed on to lend the pony to one of my messmates on the plea of sickness.

We happened to be on the move nearly the whole day, the road was bad, and my friend's conscience worse, or rather he had none, as he scarcely dismounted the animal the whole day, and the following morning I found my poor pony dead. This was one of those little circumstances that so soon teach a young soldier to look after number one. Hitherto we had continued to keep up the mess of the regiment; but at last we became so thoroughly dissatisfied with seeing nothing but salt beef, salt pork, and Dall curry on the table, that we unanimously determined to break it up and trust to our own resources; by which arrangement we considerably bettered our condition, as some three or four officers, as inclination or convenience suited, clubbed together, who were all bound to exert their utmost wit and ingenuity for their common good; and I must say, that from this time we fared much better, as it was but seldom that we did not manage by some means to secure something eatable, even though we paid twelve or fourteen rupees for a fowl—which we often did.

One day the members of the little mess to which I belonged, were lavish in their praise of one of the dishes, which my servant had put on the table for dinner, and on enquiry as to what it was, and where he had got it, he very innocently told us that he had bought part of a calf that had been taken out of a cow that was shot in the jungle; this little fact will, I think, prove how really and truly hard-pushed we were to obtain anything like fresh provisions at this time.

The 3rd of June was to me, and I believe to the greater part of the regiment, a day of high excitement. It was the day on which the first attack was made on Kemmendine, a strongly fortified stockade on the banks of the river, about four miles above Rangoon, a name that now stands pre-eminently first in the history of the Burmese war, for the gallant defence made by the Madras European regiment, and the 26th regiment Native Infantry in December 1821, when besieged by the army of the great Bundoola, as I shall hereafter have occasion to mention.

At an early hour this morning the regiment, with detachments from several of the native corps, were drawn up on the high road leading to the Great Pagoda in two columns, one commanded by Lieutenant-Colonel Smith, tile other by Lieutenant-Colonel Hodgson, for the attack of Kemmendine; a third column, composed of part of H. M.'s 41st regiment with a flotilla of gunboats under the command of Sir A. Campbell, had proceeded at an early hour for the same place by water.

At the base of the Pagoda the columns separated; Colonel Smith's division took the open or lower road, Colonel Hodgson's the upper road through the jungle; and for a couple of hours or more, we neither heard or saw any appearance of an enemy in the dark gloomy jungle that surrounded us. We began to suspect that we had lost our way, or that our guide was deceiving us; suddenly, however, our doubts were at an end, as a long wild and savage howl echoed through the wood, then ceased, only to be repeated again and again.

We now closed up our ranks and pushed on as fast as we could, and as we approached the spot from whence the war-whoop of the enemy had proceeded, we found the left column, under Colonel Smith, awaiting our arrival, in front of a stockade since called the "half-way stockade". Arrangements for the attack were soon completed, as we had no guns to breach tile works, or ladders to escalade them, and nothing but our wits to trust to—which is an article a soldier generally carries about him ready for all occasions, and which as it is not a heavy commodity, usually answers his purpose well.

There was some consultation before we advanced, as to the best means of capturing a stockade thirteen or fourteen feet high, and well garrisoned; but it was impossible to form any plan which we had the means of carrying into effect, except that of trusting in our good fortune and the bravery of our little party. The grenadier company of the regiment led the attack, and by mounting on each other's shoulders, stormed and carried the stockade in gallant style.

The light company of the regiment were employed as skirmishers to cut off the retreat of the enemy upon the Kemmendine; and as the Burmese escaped from the stockade, great numbers fell by their steady fire, but all were spared who asked for mercy, except one man, who attempted to spear the soldier who had but a minute before spared his life. Indeed the Burmese wounded him severely and then ran off; but it was not far; the soldier, who was a good marksman, levelled his piece and shot him dead.

After the capture of this stockade, the troops were again formed up in column and advanced to the attack at Kemmendine. Colonel Smith's division led the way, and took up a position to the north of the stockade, in communication with the river party under Sir A. Campbell.

Colonel Hodgson's division followed and took post on the left centre; the extreme left of the position being a thick jungle, we did not attempt to occupy it. For some time we were busily employed in cutting down bamboos to make scaling ladders, but as we had neither rope nor nails to fasten them together after we had cut them, the work was soon discontinued; indeed, it was high time to do so, for the gunboats in the river overshot the stockade, and were peppering us at a devil of a rate. Colonel Hodgson led this division to the attack, at the head of the light company of the regiment. As we passed through a bamboo hedge running parallel with the stockade, at about fifty paces distant, we were checked by a heavy fire from the rear, which, from its regularity, the colonel at once perceived came from our own troops, and consequently ordered us to lay ourselves flat on the ground, which we did, and in a short time the firing ceased, and we again advanced to the attack of the stockade.

In a few minutes nearly one-third of our party were disabled, and several men killed, and the firing from the gunboats continued to annoy us as much as it had done in our former position. At this point, the stockade was at least fifteen feet high; we were without a single scaling ladder, and exposed to a heavy and destructive fire, which we were unable to return. In this extremity the Colonel set the pioneers at work with their hatchets to cut an entrance into the stockade; but I fancy the work was too warm for them, as they soon disappeared. Nevertheless our men continued to persevere in the attempt to pull down the stockade, but it was vain and useless under so heavy a fire, and being without the means to accomplish it.

When the retreat sounded, we had lost more than a hundred men killed and wounded, including amongst the latter, two officers, Captain Kyd and Lieutenant Stinton. Fortunately the Burmese remained within the stockade and allowed us to retire quietly, or we might have suffered more severely, for it was with the greatest difficulty and exertion that we were enabled to carry off our wounded, the dooley-bearers with the conveyances for the sick and wounded, having all gone to the rear. We scarcely knew what to do, as many of our men were so badly wounded that they were unable to move, and the poor fellows begged of us not to leave them to be murdered by the Burmese. At last, I thought of a contrivance that answered very well: I seated a wounded man on a musket between two of his comrades, with his arms round their necks; and we carried them all to the half-way stockade which we had captured in the morning, where we managed to obtain some better conveyance for them. Poor Pridgeon, of the light company, I believe to be the only survivor of those carried off the field by his comrades on that day, and he is a pensioner, with only one leg to support his active body, for at that time he was not twenty years of age.

Whilst the troops were under the stockade trying to gain an entrance, Serjeant Morrison, of the light company, was dispatched to the rear with an order to bring up a small field-piece that had been left at the half-way stockade; and on his way back at the head of the party, he was shot dead by a Burmese who had secreted himself in the jungle by the roadside. Poor Morrison! He was a good soldier, and much respected by the; officers and men, and his death was lamented by us all.

I have said that we were for a considerable time close under the stockade, and that. during that time we had a great many men killed, which was the more galling as we were unable to retaliate; on one occasion Lieutenant Stinton, of the grenadier company, observed a Burmese fire once or twice from the same place, and always with a deadly aim; he kept his eye on the spot, and when he saw the fellow's musket again directed towards the party, he turned half round to order one of the men to fire at him, when on the instant of his turning round, the Burmese again fired, and the ball went through poor Stinton's seat of honour, which distressed him sadly, as he said people might fancy he had been running away; but doubtless his turning round at that instant saved his life for had the ball struck him in front, it would most probably have mortally wounded him.

After the capture of the half-way stockade, a soldier of the regiment named Mason committed an act of great barbarity, in taking the life of a poor inoffensive child, who with others had been unable to effect their escape from the stockade, and had secreted himself under a mat, where he was observed; and wantonly bayoneted; but the end of this soldier was pitiable, and was considered by his comrades as a just retribution for the perpetration of a wanton and atrocious act of cruelty. He died raving mad, from the effects of a wound on the head he received this day, after a lingering and most painful illness.

CHAPTER 6

Taking the Stop & Tiff Stockade

For several days after our return to Rangoon, active preparations were carried on for a second attack on Kemmendine, and on the 10th of June the regiment formed a part of a force of nearly three thousand men, assembled for that purpose; and in this instance every requisite of war was amply supplied: three or four eighteen-pounders, several field-pieces and mortars, and what was of greater consequence, scaling-ladders.

From the circumstance of our having no draught cattle, our progress was very slow, as the guns were dragged by working parties from the European regiments detailed for that purpose, and hard work it was, over the heavy ground on the lower road to Kemmendine. About ten o'clock the advance halted in front of a stockade, since called "Stop and tiff", within a mile of Kemmendine; and in a few minutes afterwards, Sir A. Campbell rode up to one of the battalion companies of the regiment, and said, that he wanted some volunteers for a forlorn hope. A great many men stepped forward; but Corporal Freerer was the first of them, and the General in consequence promoted him on the spot to be Serjeant.

The guns were soon brought up; but after a heavy fire

for some time, it was found that they produced but little effect, and the storming parties from H. M.'s 38th and 41st regiments, and Madras European regiment were ordered to advance with ladders to escalade, which they performed in good style, under a pretty heavy fire, H. M.'s 13th, or Bloody Blazers, as they sometimes were called, being employed to cut off the retreat of the enemy.

Major Chambers received a severe wound in the mouth, when mounting the ladders at the head of the storming party of H. M.'s 41st regiment, and Lieutenant Robertson of the Madras European regiment was also severely wounded at the head of his party, and ultimately died from the effects of his wound. On the morning of his death I went to visit him as usual, and to my surprise found that he was dead, for I was not even aware that the poor fellow's life was considered to be in danger; but I quite shuddered when I saw a cat coiled up on his breast, for I had often read accounts of these animals having attacked the dead, and I looked at the beast with indescribable abhorrence. I always disliked them as cunning and treacherous, even in their most playful moods; but the circumstance of finding this creature coiled upon the breast of the dead man, struck me as something most horrible.

CHAPTER 7

The Attack on Kemmendine

But to return to my story. After this brilliant little affair, in which the Burmese had between two and three hundred killed, the General lost no time in pushing forward to Kemmendine, a flotilla having been despatched early the same morning to prevent the escape of the Burmese on the river-side. We were received as usual with yells of defiance, which continued at intervals all night; but towards the morning they became fainter and fainter, and at daylight ceased altogether; which I shall presently account for.

Although our force was more than adequate to surround the stockade, the upper or north side was not invested, neither were, the stockades above Kemmendine any obstacle to our doing so, as has been asserted by some, for the nearest was not within half a mile of our position, and the road between the two was protected by the fire of the flotilla, which commanded the whole line of communication to the north of Kemmendine. In fact, it appeared to me, when I explored that part of the country a few days later, an unaccountable omission on the part of the General, not having occupied ground every way so advantageous, and which would have placed the enemy entirely at his mercy.

Soon after we had taken up our position in front of Kemmendine, the pioneers were set at work to erect batteries for the eighteen-pounders and mortars, within fifty paces of the stockade, protected by the light company of the regiment, which was thrown forward for that purpose; and as soon as the night set in, we crept up to our post behind some bushes within thirty paces of the stockade, not, however, unobserved by the Burmese, who saluted us whenever an opening in the jungle enabled them to get sight of any movement. Indeed our post was so close to the stockade, that our sentries were obliged to crawl upon their hands and knees to relieve each other throughout the night, as the least stir or noise on our parts was sure to be followed by a warm fire from our ever watchful enemy.

Our situation, as may easily be conceived, was none of the most enviable, as we were totally destitute of tents or cover from the rain, which fell heavily the greater part of the night, and the mosquitoes annoyed us dreadfully. Nevertheless I must have slept very soundly, as, when I awoke at daylight, I found myself several inches deep in a puddle of soft mud and water. The rain, however, had ceased, and our batteries were pounding away at a famous rate; but it proved to be to little purpose; as the bamboos were so elastic that the shot passed through them without much injury, and we were consequently rejoiced to hear the order given to escalade.

As the bugle sounded the advance, we shouldered the ladders and hastened forward, each man anxious to be the first to enter the stockade: but to our surprise and mortification we found it empty! The Burmese had wisely availed themselves of the darkness of the night, to make their escape by the passage on the north of the stockade, which, I have mentioned, was unoccupied by our troops. How they must have chuckled when they found themselves safe, and heard us for hours firing away at an empty stockade! Four companies of the regiment remained to garrison the stockade, and the rest of the force returned to Rangoon the same day.

The next morning we amused ourselves by rambling through the stockades that extend for nearly a mile along the banks of the river above Kemmendine. The enemy had disappeared, and the stockades were all deserted; but some of our men chanced to find a Burmese, who was so badly wounded, that he had been unable to make his escape with those who fled from Kemmendine the day before, and he was now suffering the most acute agony from his wound, and by signs requested us to behead him, which the men were anxious to do from sheer charity, as they said it would be a mercy to release him from the pain and misery he was suffering. But this of course was not sanctioned, although the surgeon said that nothing could save him; and whether the men carried their benevolent wishes into effect or not, I cannot tell; but they evidently felt for the poor fellow's suffering.

A detachment of the regiment from the Grenadier company, with Lieutenant Grubb as its subaltern, was sent from Kemmendine to occupy the stockade of "Stop and tiff", and the description given of the place, and the work left for our men to perform, was most disgusting.

No pioneers were left with the detachment, or pickaxes, or tools of any description supplied them wherewith to bury the dead, an operation which self defence soon rendered so imperiously necessary, that some of the bodies were burnt, and others thrown into the trenches, and covered over as they best might with loose earth. The heavy rains, however, soon washed this slight covering away, and left exposed, arms, legs, heads, &c. in all stages of putrefaction from which a most pestilent effluvia arose, that soon affected the whole detachment, and was the cause of much sickness.

CHAPTER 8

In the Lines

Shortly after our return from Kemmendine, the Burmese again made their appearance in front of our lines, and scarcely a day passed without some skirmishing with the pickets; and on one occasion they took up a position within fifty paces of our out-line picket behind a thick bamboo hedge, and annoyed us considerably. At night they frequently crawled upon their hands and knees through the high grass within a few paces of the sentries before they were perceived; and one night they actually surprised a Sergeant's picket in this manner, and the sentry was cut down before the least notice or signal of their approach was given.

I was subaltern of the inline picket on that night, and marched up my guard on the first signal of attack; but the enemy had already disappeared, and the absence of the picket, and the dead body of the sentry, were sufficient evidence of the result of the attack. The spot was surrounded by jungle and high grass, and considerably in advance of the chain of sentries from the main picket; in fact it was an insulated position, injudiciously selected; and no blame could be attached to a party surprised in such a position, by such an active enemy as we had to deal with.

Among other events at this time, I remember our surprise at receiving an order through the Adjutant, for officers of companies to inspect the messes of their men, and to report if they were in any way different from the usual dinners served out, and to ascertain if a charge made by the Commissary-general against the regiment, of having purloined one of the public draft-cattle, was correct.

I must mention that the lines of H. M.'s 41st regiment were next to ours, and this bullock was said to have been left with a public cart by its driver, for a short time, in a space between the lines of the two regiments, and that when he returned the animal was gone, and of course the fault was laid upon our corps, as the General thought it impossible that one of H. M.'s regiments could have been guilty of such an act. The aide-de-camp, in giving his orders to Colonel Kelly, said that Sir Archibald Campbell intended, should he find out that our men had killed the bullock, to send the regiment back to Madras, and report in strong terms to the Madras government his reasons for so doing. This order wore certainly an unpleasant aspect; however, as we were directed to inspect and report the result of our observations, it was done; but luckily we found nothing, and could gain no information of the theft, and the Colonel reported the same.

A week after this, when the business had blown over, we learnt that the Grenadier company of the 41st had been the culprits, and that at the time we were making the search among our men, they were enjoying a capital dish of beef, in which the officers of the company participated. The General knew of this affair afterwards, but not a word was ever mentioned in orders about them, nor was the order, threatening to disgrace our corps, ever rescinded.

CHAPTER 9

Gunboats and Rockets

In consequence of the harassing attacks made on the pickets, the General determined on sending out a large force under the-command of General MacBean, to attack the enemy, said to be strongly stockaded at Kummeroot above Kemmendine, while Sir A. Campbell, with a strong force on board the gunboats, beat up their old quarters at Pagoda Point.

There were two roads by which the land force could advance; one a mere foot-path, the other passable for guns. The General judiciously selected the foot-path, which took us to the rear of the enemy's position quite unobserved, although we distinctly heard the enemy hard at work cutting down trees for their fortification, on either side of us, in the jungle through which we passed. We had evidently come upon them by surprise, as we saw parties in all directions coming from the woods to the defence of the stockades.

Our force was halted, and formed up in column out of sight of the enemy, for the purpose of making concerted signals with Sir A. Campbell, that the attack by the river and land forces might be simultaneous. Rockets were thrown up by our party, which were soon responded to by a gun, and General MacBean then made preparations for attacking the stockades. The regiment was kept in reserve, and H. M.'s 13th and 38th regiments moved to the attack. Lieutenant Abbott of the Bengal engineers planted the ladders, and was the first to mount them, followed by the storming party, and they were soon over the walls, and a heavy fire commenced on both sides. But the attacking party proved as usual too much for them, and drove the Burmese from one stockade into another, until at last they found they could retreat no farther. Some attempted to climb over the walls, and others rushed towards the only gate through which they might hope to escape; but the greater part of them, including the Shumbah Woonghee fell, from the fire of the attacking party.

I did not go into the stockades after they were taken; but an officer of the regiment went over them, and on his return he said there must have been upwards of three hundred of the enemy killed in the last stockade, where they had been surrounded, and had made a desperate fight. He found a very good double-barrelled Manton's gun, loaded with three or four balls in each barrel, which he brought away. It was most probably the Woonghee's property, as it was lying near his body. Several stand of colours, and a great quantity of arms of all descriptions were captured; and a Tealoch, or gold chain of nine links, worn by the Woonghee, was secured by one of the soldiers, who afterwards sold it for upwards of six hundred rupees. Sir A. Campbell also succeeded in taking the Pagoda Point stockade; but with little loss to either party.

I have before said that there were two roads to this

stockade, and that General MacBean had wisely selected the bye-road. On our return to Rangoon, the regiment was ordered to proceed by the lower or main road, and to ascertain if any body of the enemy were stockaded in that direction. This, however, we were unable to accomplish, as within half a mile of the stockades we came to a deep nullah, which we were unable to cross, and which obliged us to return by the road we had come out. Some days subsequently, a party of reconnaissance was sent out to ascertain if the enemy had re-occupied these works, when they found the lower road stockaded in five or six places, but unoccupied, from which it was evident that the Burmese were well prepared to oppose our advance by that road on the 8th July, and that our advance through the jungle by a common foot-path was unexpected, and took them by surprise.

On the banks of the nullah which prevented our return by the lower road, I saw an instance of the despotic power, and barbarous cruelty exercised by the Burmese chiefs, in the crucifixion of two unfortunate Burmese; one of them had his stomach and bowels burnt out by molten lead poured down his throat, and the other was ripped up and had his heart torn out. The remainder of the month passed by without any occurrence worthy of notice, as the Burmese left us unmolested.

About the middle of last century Syriam was the most flourishing commercial town in Burmah; it is now a mere village. But the Kyk Pagoda, about two miles inland, is a strong position, which the Burmese now occupied in force, and improved by stockading; and from hence they frequently sallied forth and attacked our fishing boats, and otherwise caused us much annoyance, which the General determined to put a stop to by dispatching a force to drive the enemy from the position.

Accordingly, on the 3rd of August, a strong detachment embarked for that purpose. On landing, a heavy fire was opened on an old fort that had been stockaded, and which was soon captured; after which, the regiment advanced under the command of Colonel Kelly, to the attack of the Pagoda at Syriam, which was also carried with little loss, although the position was a strong one and well barricaded. Indeed, I do not know an instance in which the Burmese did not show great judgment in the selection of positions for defence, and it was surprising with what rapidity they erected them.

CHAPTER 10

Treachery and Ambush

About this time some Burmese came over from Dalla, with intelligence that many of the Burmese on that side of the river were anxious to come into Rangoon, and were prevented by a strong party that were unfriendly to us; but that if the General would send over a small party to their assistance, he need not apprehend any attack, as there were no troops on that side of the country, and the villagers would at once place themselves under our protection. This was what we had long anxiously hoped for, and the correctness of the present information was never for an instant doubted.

I have said that the town of Dalla was situated on the other side of the river, opposite to Rangoon. It is flanked by a large creek or nullah, which falls into the river just below the town, and our Burmese friends were said to be located on the banks of this creek, about twenty miles in the interior. The Madras European regiment, and detachments from several Native corps, were ordered on this duty; and as it was supposed they would be out for some days, they were supplied with three days' provisions. We embarked early on the morning of the 7th, crossed the river, and entered the Dalla creek, without the slightest suspicion of the enemy being near us, and consequently were not a little surprised at coming upon a stockade before we had proceeded two miles up the creek.

When the Burmese opened a heavy and well-direct-ed fire on us, our boats' crews of Lascars became panic-struck, and we had much difficulty in getting the boats to the bank of the river; but after great exertion, and sundry hard blows well administered, we succeeded, and here we found ourselves up to our waists in mud and water, as the banks of the nullah are overflowed at high tide. The ammunition of the men became nearly all damaged, we were exposed to a heavy fire, and the mud was so deep that the men literally stuck in it; and if it had not been for the exertion of the officers, who were unencumbered with arms and accoutrements, and carried up and planted the ladders, our loss must have been very great, and our success doubtful; as we were exposed to a heavy cross-fire from a second stockade not fifty yards distant, which caused us the loss of three officers, and fifty men killed and wounded, Lieutenant Grubb of the regiment being one of the latter.

As Colonel Kelly did not think himself justified in act-ing further on information that had already proved to be false, we re-crossed the river, and returned to Rangoon the same day.

One night in the early part of the month of September, heavy firing was heard in the direction of Dalla creek, and the next morning, we learnt that an attack had been made on the *Kitty* gun brig, stationed off the entrance to the creek; but she was gallantly defended by her commander, Crawford; and the prompt assistance rendered by Captain Marriott, R.N. and the boats from the shipping in the river, saved her from being captured. Her Commander and all his crew, however, were wounded, and some of them severely, as the Burmese had actually boarded the little vessel before the boats came to her assistance.

Captains of the transports lying in the river, were in the habit of sending out their boats daily to fish, up some of the numerous creeks that unite with the Rangoon river, and on several occasions they had been captured. To prevent a repetition of these daring attacks, a ruse was attempted, which, though unsuccessful, made the Burmese very cautious ever after. A small fishing-boat was sent out as usual, but at the bottom of the boat were secreted a small party of well-armed Europeans, who were directed not to show themselves till the Burmese were well alongside the boat. But the incontrollable fear and consternation of the Lascars, when the Burmese boats appeared, frustrated this well-laid scheme of retaliation, as the Burmese made off the moment they observed the Europeans, and our boats were never able to compete with the Burmese in point of swiftness.

Chapter 11

Attack on Kykloo

I was not present at the attack of Kykloo, on the 4th of October, as none but Native troops were employed on that occasion; but as it caused a great sensation at the time, I will mention the leading points as they were detailed to me by an eye-witness. The force was commanded by Lieutenant-Colonel Smith, and consisted of the 3rd and 34th light infantry. Within two miles of the Dagon Pagoda, the force came upon an extensive but unoccupied stockade, and from thence moved on to the village of Karingie, where Lieutenant and Adjutant Campbell of the pioneers was mortally wounded, after planting the scaling ladders, and while in the act of cheering a company of the 3rd Native Infantry to move to the attack. Information was here obtained of the assembly of a large force of the enemy at Kykloo five miles in advance, which induced Colonel Smith to request Sir A. Campbell to send him a reinforcement of European troops; however, none were sent; but two hundred of the 28th regiment Native Infantry arrived in camp about one o'clock, and at two the force were again on the move towards Kykloo, which they reached about five o' clock, as it was becoming dusk.

This rapid advance was said to have been occasioned

by some message which Colonel Smith received from Sir A. Campbell regarding his request for a reinforcement of Europeans; but whatever might have been the cause, the attack which followed was a complete failure, and two officers and about thirty men were left on the field, dead or dying, to the mercy of the Burmese.

On the return of this force to camp, Brigadier McCreagh was dispatched with a body of one thousand Europeans for the attack of Kykloo, but found it deserted, and the bodies of the officers and men killed on the 4th, hung up on each side of the road leading to the stockade, and horribly mutilated, Just about this time a capital retort was played off by a young ensign of the regiment, H——, upon Lieutenant-Colonel H——, of the 9th Native Infantry, which I will mention, as the Colonel thought he was showing his strict conformity to orders in reporting a circumstance that he imagined would raise him in the estimation of the Chief. But had he been more experienced in those slight digressions which occur in a campaign, he would not have been less up to his work. Your garrison martinets, however, are not always the best soldiers on service. As the affair turned out much to his chagrin and disappointment, nothing farther was heard of the report he made.

It was shortly after sunset one day, that H—— was on the out-lying picket, and some two or three officers of the regiment, in their afternoon's ramble, had dropped in to see how he was getting on, when the serjeant of the picket reported that one of the advanced sentries had passed the word, that some fine cows were quietly grazing in front, just at the verge of the jungle. Our men had been too long fed on salt junk, for H—— to lose so good an opportunity as the present for a feast of fresh beef, so invitingly offered.

Consequently a couple of good marksmen were sent out, who stole quietly up to the herd, and picked out the finest and fattest among them, which they of course killed. The butcher was now put into requisition, and having rid the animal of its entrails, they dragged it up to the picket, and commenced work immediately. By this time all hands were crowding round and feasting their eyes in anticipation on the repast which was awaiting them, when they were suddenly disturbed by some one galloping up to the picket, and exclaiming:

"Who is the officer on picket?"

On this, H—— came forward, for it proved to be no less a person than the field-officer of the day (Colonel H——), who asked what was the cause of the firing he had heard, There was no getting out of the dilemma, as the cause of the firing was then lying on the ground before his eyes; so H—— said that some cows had been grazing in front of the picket, and that as the men had been so long on salt provisions, he had allowed a couple of men to go in front and fire at them.

"Very good, sir," said the Field Officer, "you will be pleased to account for this wastage of Government ammunition when you forward your report to me in the morning, and I shall report your conduct to the officer commanding the forces"; and away he galloped.

Necessity being the mother of invention, H—— and his friends bethought themselves of what was best to be done on such an occasion, and as Brigadier M——t, of H.

M.'s 89th regiment, then commanded the Madras forces, H—— determined on sending him a choice piece of beef as the best way of finding the road to the Brigadier's heart, and preparing him for the intended report which he was to receive the following morning; and a prime bit for rump steaks was accordingly sent off that evening. The next morning, H—— forwarded his statement to the Field Officer, reporting the wastage of two rounds of ammunition, as directed, and it was forwarded on to the Brigadier, with Colonel H——'s remarks thereon.

To make all things sure, H—— put a bold face on the business, and called on the Brigadier the same day, who said jokingly as he entered:

"Very well, Mr. H——, a pretty report the Field Officer has made of you this morning, for a breach of discipline while you were on duty yesterday!"

H—— replied, that it was so good an opportunity of giving the men a little fresh provender, that he could not resist the temptation; but hoped at the same time that the beef had proved good, which was responded to by the Brigadier in his usual affable manner, and ended by his asking H—— to stay and partake of it.

CHAPTER 12

Garrisoned

In November it fell once more to my lot to be stationed at Kemmendine, which at this time was garrisoned by a detachment of artillery, the Madras European regiment, and the 26th Madras Native Infantry, under the command of Major Yates of the latter corps.

Of course I found it in a more habitable state than when I was last stationed there, immediately after the capture of the place; and a pleasant time I now passed there, with nothing to do but amuse myself. I took advantage of the kindness of my commandant, Major Yates, to explore the country all round for miles, and I was well rewarded for my pains, as I found out a large range of gardens in the vicinity of the seven stockades, some miles above Kemmendine, full of the most delicious fruit of every description. That all might participate in this piece of good luck, a party of us went out nearly every day for a fresh supply, for there was an abundance; but this did not last long, as on one occasion we found the gardens which we had frequented only a few days before, stripped of every thing—which we could not account for, as we were quite sure that we had not left them in that state.

On consulting with Lieutenant Reynolds of the 26th,

who had accompanied me, we determined on pushing on farther into the jungle, to ascertain if there were not other gardens near, from which we might obtain our wonted supply. Reynolds and myself took the lead, followed by the few of our party who were armed, more than half of those who were with us having come out in their undress merely to bring in the fruit. Indeed, I don't think that we ever thought of falling in with an enemy: however, we were mistaken; for within half a mile of the gardens we had quitted, we came suddenly upon a large house, so completely shut out from view by the surrounding jungle that we were within twenty paces of it before Reynolds and myself observed it.

At first we only saw one man, and he was quietly cooking his rice underneath tile house; but as we advanced, he caught sight of us, when he gave a yell that brought his comrades out in double quick, tumbling over one another, and head over heels, in the greatest consternation; and although we immediately pushed forward, they were too quick for us. Reynolds, who had a double-barrelled gun on his shoulder, said, as the last fellow was making off, "Shall I shoot him?" But the poor fellow was unarmed and running away, so we let him get off. They were so completely taken by surprise, that they left all their arms behind them, swords, muskets, spears, e. in abundance, which I was certainly by no means sorry for, as more than half our party were unarmed, and we were at least five or six miles from Kemmendine, the road to which was nothing more than a foot path with a dense jungle on either side; and hearing the shouts of the enemy on every side, and not knowing how numerous they might be, I was heartily glad when my little party reached Kemmendine again in safety.

The following day, a strong force was sent out on a reconnaissance, but nothing more was seen of the enemy; they had decamped. My small detachment ought to have been relieved on the 15th, but in accordance with Major Yates' wish, as we had no objection, Sir A. Campbell granted his request that we might be allowed to remain at Kemmendine till the end of the month. This, to me, was delightful; I was in the midst of friends, for the officers of the 26th regiment were a fine liberal set of fellows, and the kindness of Major Yates, who commanded that regiment, to myself on all occasions, I shall never forget. And then, the excitement of the life I was leading, made me rejoice at being detained at Kemmendine; but as soon as this was known, the captain of my company, who was with the regiment at Rangoon, wrote me word that the corps was ordered to Pegue, and he was sure that I should be mortified to find that myself and he would be left behind in consequence of my being detained at Kemmendine.

I was excited beyond measure; I scarcely knew what I did; but I was determined that I would not be left behind, and that my friend should not suffer on my account; and although it was not seven o'clock in the morning, I rushed over to the Major's quarters, and I think he must have thought me mad from the vehemence with which I urged my request that he would get me relieved. But when I showed him my friend's letter, he said, "Be quiet, and don't excite yourself; I will do all I can for you, although I scarcely know how to get you relieved after having applied for you to remain; but I will do my best, though I shall be very sorry to lose you." He did apply and I was relieved, and went with my company to Pegue, but that was not till the end of the month, and some days after I had returned to Rangoon.

At this time, those who had coin began to fare somewhat better, as several ships had lately arrived from Calcutta with fresh stores and supplies, which were selling at the modest rate of ten rupees for a fowl, and thirty or forty rupees, viz. three or four pounds, for a sheep, bought at Calcutta for two and three rupees. But to those who valued health more than their pockets, and who had the means, it was an opportunity of recruiting that was seized on with avidity; and, as I said, we now fared much better, and were really able to indulge our hungry stomachs with a little fresh provision occasionally.

A very ludicrous affair happened one night to two of our officers, when returning from a vessel they had been dining on board of. The captain had given them a fine sucking pig to bring on shore, which was a great prize; while we had nothing but salt junk for our daily rations. The officers were, at the time I speak of, Captain K—— and Lieutenant F——; and after landing, they made the best of their way to our lines, K—— with the pig under his arm. They had no difficulty in passing through the Sepoy lines; but as soon as they approached ours, they were challenged by a sentry, who instantly came to the charge. K—— answered "friend", and was going to pass on, when the sentry demanded the parole, which they did not know, but K—— thought he would be able to pass by asking the man if he did not know he was Captain of his company. The sentry still kept his musket at the charge, and said, *that might be, but he could not let him pass without receiving the parole.* All this time the pig was squeaking at a great rate, and although K—— held him tight by the snout he managed to make a woeful noise, and as K—— perceived that the-sentry was determined to observe his orders, he was obliged to go back to the in-lying picket of the 41st, to ask the parole to get into his own lines. This must have been nuts to crack, to the sentry—making his own Captain return for the parole.

CHAPTER 13

The Pegue Expedition

On the 27th of November, the regiment, with a detachment of Native troops, under the command of Lieutenant-Colonel Mallet, of H. M.'s 89th regiment, embarked in row-boats for Pegue, supported by Captain Chadds, R.N. with some men-of-war boats. Our progress was slow; but the weather was fine, and the change enjoyed by all. We passed the ruins of a large pagoda on the banks of the river, where doubtless a town had once existed; but now all was desolate. At the small village of Obo, we halted for a short time; and as the boats came up, we were told to disembark the men without their arms and accoutrements, which was done, and they were soon scattered all over the village; but to guard against our being surprised, the Colonel ordered me to proceed to the outskirts of the village, and report immediately if I saw any appearance of an enemy.

The poor villagers were running off to the jungle with their children, and the little property they had hastily gathered up, in the greatest consternation. I tried to secure a stout hale fellow whom I found lurking in some bushes close to the village; but before we could overtake him, he jumped into a large tank, frightened nearly out of his wits, and no persuasion on our parts would induce him to come out; doubtless he afterwards told, a marvellous tale of his narrow escape.

The following day we landed at a long, straggling village, on the banks of the river opposite the Shoe Madoo Pagoda at Pegue, which we saw about a mile off. No opposition was offered to our landing; indeed, we scarcely saw a human being, and not a single stockade; the country was desolate, and the town deserted. Of the ancient and once celebrated town of Pegue, the pagoda is now the sole vestige.

On the 30th of November the troops re-embarked, and with the current in our favour, we glided down the river at a great rate, and by sunrise on the morning of the 2nd of December, we found ourselves once more in sight of the noble Shoe Dagon Pagoda, at Rangoon. We were not a little surprised to hear that our lines from the stockade to the Pagoda, were besieged by a countless army under the command of the great Bundoola,—the very thing that we could have most ardently prayed for, as it brought us face to face with our enemies; and a fair field and no favour was all we wanted; as we never for an instant doubted the result of a contest in the open plain, notwithstanding the disparity of numbers; for at this time our hospitals were still crowded with sick, and one half of our army were little better than convalescent.

CHAPTER 14

The Siege of Kemmendine

Kemmendine was also besieged, and the most determined efforts of the enemy were directed towards that point, The following narrative of this siege from the pen of an officer of the regiment, who was eye-witness, and participated in the gallant defence made by the little garrison at Kemmendine for nine days without intermission, will, I am sure, be read with interest:

> At the stockade of Kemmendine, were stationed the 26th regiment Native infantry commanded by Major Yates, a detachment of the Madras European regiment, and a detail of European artillery and Galundauze. At the distance of nearly a mile above Kemmendine, was a projecting point of land, which divided the Panlang from the Tantabeen Creek. This was called Pagoda Point by us, from the circumstance of there being a pagoda built on it. A company's cruiser, the *Thetis*, commanded by Captain Goodrich of the Bombay Marines, was stationed at the junction of these creeks, to prevent the Burmese war-boats from annoying the force at Kemmendine, or floating down fire rafts on the shipping in the river.

In consequence of Sir A. Campbell's having received information that a large force was collecting in the neighbourhood, a reconnoitring party under the command of Captain Rose of H. M.'s. 89th regiment, was despatched in the direction of Tantabeen to gain the desired intelligence of what was going on. They returned on the afternoon of the 30th of November; and Captain Rose reported having come upon the Burmese in large force, a few miles up the Tantabeen creek: he thought, from the preparations going on, that they intended an attack on Kemmendine. No doubt remained, that from the number of war-boats and fire rafts collected together, an attack was meditated, and Major Yates, who commanded the little garrison of Kemmendine, immediately ordered out a party of reconnaissance to ascertain if the enemy were in the immediate vicinity of the stockade; but no intelligence was gained, as, with the exception of a few elephant tracks, no indication of an enemy was observed.

The small force at Kemmendine was by no means inactive in making preparations for the expected attack. Major Yates gave directions, that before nightfall every man should be told off to his particular post, as, from the nature of our position, great vigilance was necessary to prevent a surprise, as the Burmese could advance to within fifty paces of our position under cover of the jungle, without being observed. Having few Europeans at his disposal, (for at this time only eighty-seven rank and file of the regiment were present at Kemmendine, although shortly after, they were reinforced to more than double the number,) and it being perfectly practicable to be attacked on all sides, Major Yates thought it expedient to intermix them with the Sepoys, that they might impart additional confidence to his men during the attack; and it was a wise measure, as the result proved.

Captain Robson of the 26th regiment commanded the front face of the stockade with a proportionate number of Europeans and Sepoys; Captain Reahe the north side; Captain Gordon the south; Lieutenant Aldritte of the artillery, with two twelve-pound carronades and one fieldpiece, the river face; Ensigns Hill and Weir of the regiment were stationed on the front, and north side. These preparations were completed before the evening closed in, when the men were ordered to their posts, and one-half of them permitted to lie down to take their rest fully accoutred, while the others kept watch.

The night passed off with scarcely a challenge being heard; but before the day began to break, the river above Kemmendine suddenly became illuminated by an immense mass of moving fire, and it was a grand sight as raft after raft came floating down towards us, blazing high and brilliantly. Every now and then, we saw men flitting about like demons around the fires, which hissed and cracked again as fresh combustibles were heaped on. But the most imposing part of the scene was a battery of war-boats that followed close upon the rafts, presenting in the glare of the fires a most formidable appearance.

These fire rafts are made of large beams of timber and bamboos tied together loosely, so that if the mass came athwart a ship's bows, it would swing round and encircle her. On this platform is placed every sort of combustible; firewood, and petroleum or earth-oil, (which abounds in Burmah, and ignites almost as quickly as gunpowder and slightly explodes on being fired) being the principal materials.

I have said that Captain Goodrich was stationed above Kemmendine in command of the *Thetis*. On the appearance of the fire rafts, which seemed to him too formidable an opponent to be encountered, he thought his position no longer safe, and we saw him float past Kemmendine on his way to Rangoon, leaving us to our fate. During this short space of time (about ten minutes), not a word was heard among us in the stockade; everyone felt the scene before us to be a grand and imposing spectacle; the whole jungle was illuminated, the Golden Pagoda at Rangoon, and every thing round about us, was as clearly visible as at noon day; but this pause of admiration and astonishment was over as soon as the war-boats came abreast of the stockade, and commenced firing on us.

At the same time, we became aware that the enemy had also established themselves in the jungle, and had surrounded the stockade. However, a well-directed fire from the guns, which Lieutenant Aldritte kept up with good effect, soon compelled the enemy to withdraw their war-boats to their former rendezvous above Kemmendine. On the land side the enemy appeared to be collecting in large masses, but they did not expose themselves, or seem inclined to begin the attack; and soon after, we saw them commence entrenching themselves on all sides, which they continued till they had completely invested the stockade, in defiance of a constant fire that we kept up on their working parties, which by-the-bye they returned with some effect.

After passing Kemmendine, the fire rafts floated on till they were brought up by a bend in the river, where they ran aground and burnt themselves out about midday, when Captain Goodrich, in the *Thetis*, again made his appearance, and Major Yates hailing the captain, told him, that by his having dropped down the river, the stockade had been left very much exposed to the fire of the enemy's war-boats, and that the whole of our artillery force was required to repel the enemy's attack on the land side.

As night came on, our anxiety increased, for the Burmese gongs were heard in every direction of the jungle, to collect their forces, evidently for an attack; and about eight o'clock, their long and wild howl rang far and loud through the surrounding wilderness, and then died away, only to be repeated again and again. This was the signal for their advance, which was effected in silence until they approached near to the stockade; but not a shot was fired by us, until they came within thirty paces, when an incessant and heavy fire was poured in upon them, which eventually obliged them to retreat. They had advanced in immense numbers with the intention of escalading, and were for some time close under our works, before they were beat off; and no farther attempt was made that night.

Our party slept by their arms, and were prepared for any fresh attack, as not a man quitted his post; but from this attack having been carried on close to the stockade, there was a good deal of firing from the sentries throughout the night, at those who were evidently engaged in removing the wounded from under the walls of the stockade. The night was dark and the flashes from the musketry, during the attack, were so incessant and vivid that we easily saw from one side of the stockade to the other.

The next morning we perceived that the Burmese had advanced their trenches to within fifty paces of the stockade; and as they had thrown up the earth before them, they were comparatively safe from our fire, which they returned with a true and steady aim from behind these entrenchments, annoying us greatly, as we had no battery from which we could bring our artillery to bear on them. It was therefore deemed advisable to knock down part of a small pagoda on the front face, and convert it into a battery for one of the carronades, which was soon accomplished, as the space was small; but we had scarcely fired a couple of rounds, before two of the gunners were severely wounded, and the battery was so confined, that the men were unable to work the gun properly; in consequence of which, one of the Galundauze had both his arms blown off while ramming home the cartridge. This was rather disheartening; but still the gunners persevered, until Major Yates saw that it was a sacrifice of life to no purpose, and ordered them to discontinue firing until the post could be made secure for those working the gun, which could only be effected at night; Serjeant Bond, of the regiment, however, stepped forward and requested permission to make another attempt before it was given over; but he had scarcely mounted the platform and commenced work, when he was wounded by a shower of balls from the enemy. It was certain death to him if he remained, and he was instantly ordered to come down; but his fate was sealed; another volley laid him dead beside the gun he was serving. He was a gallant soldier, and beloved by the men of his company.

During the whole of this day, the enemy kept up a heavy fire on our position, and at night they again renewed their attack as before, and attempted to force their way into the stockade with the utmost perseverance and determination. Three times they were beaten back, and as often rallied and renewed the charge with the most terrific yells; and we could plainly perceive by the flashes of the musketry that they carried ladders for the purpose of escalading. But it was to no purpose; our little party were too much for them; they were beaten off the third time with great loss, and they never attempted to renew the attack that night, although as on the former occasion, we were kept on the alert all night by small parties who made their appearance every now and then close to the stockade, searching for their killed and wounded.

At the time the enemy assaulted the stockade on the land side, we saw the river again covered with fire rafts, and war-boats, as on the night before; but Captain Goodrich never attempted to keep his station, but again dropped down the river, leaving us exposed to make the best defence we could. The result I have already mentioned. On the third day we were rejoiced to receive a reinforcement of eighty men from the regiment, which enabled us to send our wounded to Rangoon, as there was no spot in the stockade where they were not much exposed to the enemy's fire. An unfortunate accident occurred in landing this party. As one of the men attempted to jump on shore, his foot slipped, and he fell into the river and was drowned by the weight of his accoutrements and sixty rounds of ammunition, which each man carried.

Partial firing was continued throughout the next day, and the Burmese made another attack at night, but it was not so determined as on the former occasions, and they were consequently soon beaten off. Corporal Lucas, of the regiment, was noticed on several occasions during the siege for his gallantry and daring; and as he was a good marksman, he was placed behind the top of a pagoda to watch the motions of the Burmese, who were in the habit of getting into the trees, from whence they fired with a sure and deadly aim at those who happened to be moving about in the stockade. The situation of the corporal was by no means enviable, as he was struck more than once by the fire of the enemy; but this only made him more careful and keen in his look-out, and the moment he caught sight of a Burmese on any of the trees, his shot was sure to tell with effect. His name was mentioned by Major Yates, in his official report of the siege, and he well deserved it, as he was a gallant soldier.

This day the Burmese planted a small gun

within fifty paces; of the front face of the stockade, opposite a small gateway, which annoyed us
greatly; and Captain Page was ordered to make
a sortie with a party of Europeans, supported
by a company of the 26th regiment, to dislodge
the enemy, and if possible capture the gun. The
exit from the stockade was by a small gateway
just sufficient to admit of one at a time passing
out; and before twenty men had got clear of the
stockade, they were ordered to advance without
waiting to form up, and before the remainder of
the party had time to get clear of the stockade
to support them: the consequence was, that the
few men who reached the trenches, found themselves surrounded by a host of the enemy, and
were nearly all killed or wounded; and, as often
happens when those who lead a sortie show neither judgment nor foresight, the men under their
command lost all confidence; and now the word
"retreat" being suddenly passed up from the rear,
every man thought his neighbour was going to
leave him, and back they all rushed to the stockade, leaving the dead behind them.

Lieutenant Smith, of the 26th regiment, was
one of the first who was dangerously wounded through the body, and as he found himself
scarcely able to stand, and without support or assistance, he at once returned to the stockade, and
I have no doubt but that circumstance added to
the confusion, and very possibly to the idea that

a retreat had been ordered. For some time after this, our men used to say they had been accustomed to be told to "come on" not "go on", and certainly 'twas a lamentable piece of soldiership.

The Burmese still kept to their trenches, and continued to harass us greatly; and the Sepoys had not even time to cook their rice. But with all their privations, they were indefatigable and determined in defending their post; and several who had received flesh wounds would not go into hospital, but returned to their duty, after having been attended to by the surgeon. There was also an excellent feeling existing between them and our men, with whom they appeared proud to associate wherever there was any danger.

Our wounded were again sent to Rangoon, and we received a reinforcement of fifty men from the regiment, which was a great addition to our small party, as the Burmese had brought another gun to bear, and this night they again renewed their attack on the stockade with a determined perseverance and daring, equal to any of their former attempts, but just as unsuccessfully; as our fire was so heavy and well directed, that in defiance of their utmost efforts, they were unable to hold their ground for any length of time, and though they were rallied again and again, it was always with the same result.

I have mentioned that from the first, we received no assistance from the *Thetis*, as Captain

Goodrich always quitted his post when the Burmese and their fire rafts made their appearance, leaving us exposed to the attack of the enemy on the river side, which compelled Major Yates to report the circumstance to Sir A. Campbell, as our men were now almost overpowered by the fatigue of such constant and harassing duty. And at the next flow of the tide, we were glad to see H. M.'s brig *Sophie* come to our aid. Her commander, Captain Ryves, landed to communicate with Major Yates on the best manner of employing his vessel, and it was determined that whenever the Burmese attacked the stockade, blue lights should be thrown upon the side on which the enemy were assembled, when the guns from his vessel were to open on their position.

The captain had not long to wait for an opportunity of trying the effect of his fire; as, in the course of the evening, the Burmese gongs gave notice that preparations were making for another attack; and at the usual hour, yell after yell gave notice of their approach. In a short time we had to throw up blue lights on all sides of the stockade, to show that the enemy were about us on every quarter, when the captain opened the fire of his guns with excellent effect, and the roar of cannon and incessant pealing of musketry for a half hour or more was quite deafening. It gradually ceased, and then died away; and presently after we observed the river covered with the enemy's fire rafts, and, as usual, the *Thetis* dropping down in front of them. But Captain Ryves sent his first lieutenant on board her, to tell Captain Goodrich, that if he could not make any further use of his vessel as a ship of war, that he must nevertheless remain at his post, to receive the troops on board in case they should be obliged to abandon the stockade. As the rafts came floating down the river, they were with some difficulty turned off from the *Thetis*, and although Captain Ryves had his boats manned and supplied with grappling irons, he could not prevent their coming in contact with his vessel which set fire to the rigging, but it was fortunately soon extinguished, and without much injury.

The next day, the 7th, the fire of the Burmese was very slack and partial; they still, however, kept to their trenches, although they made no attack that night, and the 8th was a counterpart of the day before. On the 9th, it was evident from the firing having ceased, that they had at length taken themselves off, in despair of making any impression on our post; and thus ended the siege of Kemmendine.

No troops could have behaved better than the little force at Kemmendine, and they deserve every praise for their patient and cheerful endurance of fatigue, privations, and dangers, seldom surpassed by the best troops in the world; but it will scarcely be credited that the honour of bearing "Kemmendine" on its colours, has been withheld from the Madras European regiment, on the plea that only part of the regiment was present. Nevertheless this part was more than half the strength of the regiment.

This honour has only been conferred on the 26th regiment Native Infantry, and well do they merit the distinction, as no regiment could have behaved with greater gallantry and credit to themselves than the 26th regiment throughout the siege.

The Resolution passed by the Right Honourable the Governor in Council, conferring the honour is as follows:

26th January, 1825

Resolution

In testimony of the exemplary valour and steadiness displayed by the 26th regiment Madras Native Infantry, under the command of Major Yates, in defence of the post of Kemmendine, near Rangoon, against the furious and reiterated attacks of vastly superior numbers of the enemy by day and night, during the period between the 1st and 9th of December 1824, the Right Honourable the Governor in Council resolves that that corps shall be permitted to bear the word "Kemmendine" inscribed on their colours, as a perpetual record of their distinguished and persevering valour on that occasion.

CHAPTER 15

The Great Attack

I have said that the regiment landed at the wharf by the river side, on its return from Pegue, early in the morning of the 2nd of December, where we found our lines besieged by the Burmese; and as the aid of our small force was much required, we were forthwith marched off to our lines, and from thence to the advanced posts of the pagoda, and white-house picket, facing the village of Poossundoon, where we saw the enemy collected in immense masses throwing up entrenchments, which they never ceased to work at until they completed their lines from the village of Poossundoon to the pagoda, a distance of between two and three miles. This work, however, was no interruption to more active warfare; and their shot often penetrated the roof of our picket-house, and sent the tiles rattling about our ears, which kept us constantly on the alert.

The Burmese chiefs, with their gilt chattahs, were conspicuous throughout the day, inciting their men to renewed exertion; but it was not till the night of the 3rd, that any serious attack was made on our lines, and then it was principally directed towards the Great Dagon Pagoda. The night was intensely dark, but a confused hollow murmur, that sounded like the distant hum of many voices, convinced us that a multitude were congregated in front of our position for some desperate attack. Not a word was spoken by our little party; every man was at his post, listening with the greatest anxiety for the approach of the enemy; and that we might not be taken by surprise, a party of fifty men were posted in advance of the picket, to give us timely notice in case the enemy should creep up unawares.

In this state me remained listening intently for the slightest sound that might warn us of the approach of the enemy, until about ten o'clock, when yell after yell rang from one extremity of the enemy's lines to the other, and was succeeded by a heavy and incessant fire from the pagoda; and it was evident that the enemy had made a desperate assault on that point, which we fully expected they would follow up by an attack on our position; but in the course of an hour the firing ceased, and all was quiet again. We saw no more of the enemy that night, and the following morning we learnt that a most gallant and spirited attack had been made on the pagoda, but the enemy were beaten off after repeated attempts to escalade the works, for which purpose they appeared to have been well supplied with scaling ladders, as they left several behind them.

The morning of the 4th passed off quietly without any further attempt on our lines, although the enemy's trenches were still occupied in as great force as ever; and at night we were rejoiced to receive an order to hold ourselves in readiness to attack the enemy's entrenchments the following morning, as Sir A. Campbell had now determined on showing the Great Bundoola that we were as capable of attacking our enemies, as of defending ourselves.

Soon after daybreak on the morning of the 5th, the force stationed at the white-house picket, about six hundred bayonets, moved off in column of companies, and within a hundred paces of the enemy's entrenchments the force closed to the front, and deployed into line, under a heavy and well directed fire from the enemy, which killed our commanding officer, Lieutenant-Colonel Walker, and was the cause of some delay, during which we were exposed to a galling fire which annoyed us greatly; but not a shot was fired by our little party until the bugles sounded the advance, when the whole line rushed forwards, and drove the enemy from their entrenchments at the point of the bayonet.

To our left was a battery with a twelve pound carronade, round which the Burmese rallied, and opened a heavy fire on the rear of our force, as it advanced in pursuit of the enemy; but a charge made by the light company of the regiment, soon cleared the battery and captured the gun, which we spiked, and again charged the enemy, who had now rallied in considerable strength behind a breastwork within their entrenchments.

As I sprang on the top of this work, I found myself alone and within a few paces of a large body of the enemy; but my little party were close by, and I turned half round to urge them on, when I received a severe wound, and before I had recovered from the shock, the Burmese were driven almost out of sight; for our little force were still hotly in pursuit of the enemy, and as I soon found it useless to attempt to overtake them, I determined to return to the picket, and was accompanied by a havildar of the 34th regiment, who was also severely wounded.

We had, however, scarcely gone a quarter of a mile, when my servant, who had accompanied me throughout the day, seized me by the arm, and called out that the Burmese were coming; and true enough they were; for at no great distance, I saw the Gassy horse coming down upon us as fast as their little horses could carry them, and there appeared but small hope of our being able to escape them. Nevertheless we determined to do our best. I called out to the havildar to come along, and for some time he kept up pretty well; but we were both very weak, and could make but little progress; and as the enemy neared us, the poor havildar dropped more in the rear, and as I turned round to urge him on, I saw the Burmese ride over him.

At this moment a heavy shower of grape-shot came whistling through the air, and a well directed fire on the enemy was continued by Lieutenant Onslow, the artillery officer, in charge of the picket, at the same time that he dispatched a party of artillery men to my assistance, and in a few minutes I was safe. The Gassy horse fell back, and I saw no more of them, although at one time they were so close, that any bold fellow might have dashed out, and have cut me down, long before assistance could have reached me. My escape was entirely owing to the well directed fire opened on the enemy at that critical moment; and to Lieutenant Onslow I certainly am indebted for my life.

The poor havildar was shortly after brought in alive, but very severely wounded. But although he ultimately recovered he was unfit for duty, and retired on the pension establishment. He afterwards said, that as he saw it was impossible for us both to get off, he had stayed behind to divert the attention of the Burmese, and give me time to make my escape.

A soldier of the regiment had also a very narrow escape from the same body of Gassy horse this day. He was alone, and considerably in rear of the column, when he found himself surrounded; but whenever they approached him, he levelled his musket, and they wheeled off, merely throwing their spears at him from a distance, and this continued for some time before he was observed, and a party sent to his rescue. On being complimented on his coolness and presence of mind in not firing his musket, he said, "Oh! The b—y b—h wouldn't go off". It was evident that he owed his safety to the impression of the enemy that his musket was loaded.

A simultaneous attack on the enemy's lines was also made from the great pagoda, in which part of the regiment was also engaged; the enemy were routed in every direction, and pursued a considerable distance on the road to Kokeen. Indeed, success appeared to be complete, and so satisfied was Sir Archibald Campbell that the Burmese were totally routed, and that they would not be able to rally their troops for a fresh attack, as most of their guns, jingalls, and working implements had fallen into our hands, that his parole for that night was "victory", and the countersign "complete".

However, he soon ascertained that he was deceived, for the Great Bundoola managed to assemble his troops again in large numbers, and showed a determination to keep his ground as long as he was able, and if possible fulfil his promise to the king of Ava, that he would drive the English rebels into the sea; but as Jonathan would say, *I guess he found it a tarnation hard job.*

CHAPTER 16

Victory at Rangoon

On the evening of the 7th the regiment were rowed across the river to the *Fort William*, anchored off the entrance to the Dalla Creek, where they remained until about two o'clock that night, when they again advanced with the intention of surprising the enemy who still continued stockaded in great force at Dalla. This, however, was in a great measure frustrated in consequence of a heavy fire being opened on them before the troops were ready to take advantage of their consternation. Nevertheless they made but slight resistance, and we captured all their works without much loss on either side; and here we halted till about mid-day of the 8th, when we again moved forward to the attack of a long line of stockades and breast-works farther up the river, all of which were eventually captured after a hard day's work; for the enemy here fought well, and kept up a warm and unceasing fire with jingalls and musketry as we advanced.

One fellow made himself very conspicuous by his daring, as he stood on the top of one of these breast-works, shouting defiance, and hurting spears at all who approached him; and as Captain Roy of the regiment was leading on his party to the attack, he threw a spear at him, which entered the crown of his cap, and came out behind, grazing the back of his head: as poor Roy said, it was a precious narrow escape; but it was not the only one he had, being twice wounded that day, besides getting knocked down by a Burmese with a large stone. Lieutenant Clover of the 8th regiment Native Infantry, was also severely wounded, and was obliged to have his right arm amputated at the shoulder.

On the night of the 14th the town of Rangoon was set on fire in several places, which consumed nearly one-half of the houses, and there was no doubt but that the deed was perpetrated by the Burmese located within the stockade. At the same time, innumerable fire rafts were floated down on the shipping in the river; but fortunately the wind lulled, and the fires were extinguished before they communicated with the magazines; but a great quantity of private stores were destroyed, and the whole of the mess supplies belonging to our regiment, amounting in value to about five thousand rupees.

The following morning the whole of the disposable force moved out under the command of Sir A. Campbell for the attack of the enemy's position at Kokeen within a few miles of Rangoon, where Bundoola had concentrated the whole of his forces since their late defeat, in two stockades about three miles in circumference, on a rising ground, and of great strength. H. M.'s 13th regiment were ordered to attack the enemy's entrenchments on the reverse flank, and the remainder of the force being divided into two columns, headed by a detachment of pioneers carrying the ladders, the advance sounded, and in a short time the stockades were carried at every point, under a heavy and well directed fire, from which we suffered severely, particularly H. M.'s 13th, who were exposed to a crossfire, and had three officers and seventy men killed and wounded, although they had not quite two hundred men present.

The loss of the enemy was considerable, but not so much as it might have been, and would have been, if we had had a sufficiency of scaling ladders; and as it was, one of them broke, which delayed us still more; and before one-half of the force had entered the stockade, the greater part of the enemy had disappeared, as from the want of ladders only two of the storming party could enter together: had the enemy made a determined resistance, our loss must have been very great. Private Tate was promoted to be a Corporal in the regiment, for his gallantry on this day, particularly for the promptness with which he assisted Captain Roy to carry up and plant one of the scaling ladders, after the greater part of the pioneers and their officers had been wounded.

After the capture of the stockades at Kokeen, and the consequent dispersion of Bundoola's army the enemy disappeared altogether from the neighbourhood of Rangoon, and nothing of interest occurred until the advance of the army towards Amerapoorah in February, 1825. The troops destined for this service were divided into two columns; one to proceed by land, under the command of Sir A. Campbell in person; the other by water, commanded by General Cotton, composed of one hundred and fourteen rank and file of H. M.'s 41st regiment, one hundred and forty-four of H. M.'s 89th, two hundred and eighty-one of the Madras European regiment, and two hundred and thirty-six of the 18th regiment Native Infantry, supported by the men-of-war boats and the *Diana* steam-vessel, under the directions of Captain Alexander, R.N. On the morning of the 14th, the land column marched out to Maingaladoon, and three days afterwards, General Cotton moved off with the other division.

CHAPTER 17

Donabew

I have said that I received a severe wound on the fifth of December, and from that date I was unable to participate in the active service in which the regiment continued to be engaged; but the following account, kindly furnished me by an officer, who continued with the regiment until its departure from Burmah, as well as numerous extracts from the letters of another officer of the regiment, give a clear and detailed account of the services of the corps until the completion of the war, and will I am sure be read with interest. Of the letters, I need only say that they were written by a friend, whose memory I shall never cease to cherish with the greatest affection to the last day of my existence, and whose high and noble qualities endeared him no less to the regiment, whose honour he always upheld, and whose interest he never ceased to advocate. He was a gallant soldier, a high principled, religious man, and a warm and steady friend.

On the 15th of January, my friend writes—

"We are getting heartily tired of so inactive a life, and I fear that we shall yet have to wait some time before the preparations will be completed for an advance to Amerapoorah. It is true there was a little fighting on the 11th at Sgriam, but the regiment was not there; the party sent was from H. M.'s 47th regiment, under the command of Colonel E——, who were all new hands, and they bungled the business sadly, and suffered a heavy loss. This too was all at the small breast-work at the riverside where they halted; and the next morning found the pagoda deserted, with the exception of three or four fellows, who were left to fire off some wooden guns. The men were kept too long under the enemy's fire for some useless formations; and it was said that a similar party of old stockaders would have taken the place in a few minutes, and probably with half the loss they sustained; indeed, you know we have twice before carried the same position with very little loss.

"This reminds me of an anecdote told of Colonel G——, who was an exceedingly smart officer, and when told of the punctilious manner observed in the directions given for advancing against the place, and the consequent delay which it occasioned, replied:

"'Gad, sir, why did they not take the place first, and then give their orders?'

"You will be disgusted with the General's bombastical despatches of the 8th and 9th; those of the 5th we have not yet seen, but in them I trust he has paid a little more attention to truth, and that he has had some regard for the merits of others, instead of making his own name appear so conspicuous. If he had merely given a plain narrative of what actually occurred, the public would have been able to form a correct opinion of the business, and would have given him as well as his army much greater credit, than they will now obtain.

"If it was a matter of any consequence, the regiment would have just cause to be annoyed; as he has studiously avoided ever mentioning it, but it is well known to have been conspicuously forward on the 5th, 9th and 15th; and it will be by the opinions prevalent here, and not by exaggerated and distorted reports written to serve some particular purpose, that the merits of corps as well as individuals, will be eventually judged of. An army of 30,000 men is said to have collected again between this and Prome; but we have as usual so many contradictory reports, that we do not know which to believe. At all events, it is to be hoped that we shall be able to give a good account of them; and it is probable we shall take up our monsoon quarters at Prome; but I see no chance of the war being finished before the rains, and by that time, I fear the regiment will be completely done up, as we have already lost three hundred and seventeen men; twenty-five have returned to Madras, sixty-six have gone to Mergue, and sixty more are going there.

"The scene was novel and exhilarating as we

proceeded up the river, although our prowess was not called into action until we reached Pan-lang on the 19th, when some show of resistance was made by the enemy to our hitherto quiet progress. From the steam-vessel a few rockets were thrown into the nearest stockade, which set fire to some of the houses, on which the enemy immediately deserted their position.

"At a bend of the river, however, there was still another large and formidable stockade un-captured, divided from the former by a creek some sixty or seventy yards broad, and we were all confounded when the General stated his in-tention of fording the creek, and called out, "Fol-low me!". In we dashed, the men carrying their pouches on their bayonets; but some, who were short and stout, soon lost their footing and were only saved from drowning by the grenadiers; and when we reached the opposite bank, we had still to wait for the gunboats before we could attack the stockade; and after all we found the Burmese had deserted it, So much for Sir Willoughby's playing the part of a Captain of Grenadiers."

On the 16th of March, my friend writes from Don-abew—

"Since I wrote to you from Panlang, we had made but little progress, owing to Sir Archibald's having gone on past Donabew, where, accord-ing to the original plan, he was to have joined

us; leaving a handful of us to dispose of Bundoola, who is stockaded here in an immensely
strong position, and has collected from twelve
to fifteen thousand of the best troops of the empire, with two hundred pieces of cannon, three
hundred jingalls, and five or six thousand muskets, besides seventy elephants, and one thousand
Gassy horse. However, to give you an idea of all
our operations, I must go back to Panlang. We
moved from thence on the 25th, leaving twenty-
five of our men, and the 18th N. I. to garrison
the place under the command of Major Ross.
On the 27th we entered the Irrawaddy without
material opposition, at Yangain-chingah, which
is merely a paltry village.

"Here we remained until the 5th, when all
the boats that had been despatched to Panlang for
provisions having come up, we again moved on
towards Donabew. I had the honour of being tak-
en on board the steam-vessel with part of the light
company. She had four large brigs, and five or six
boats in tow, and it was a fine sight to see her
move majestically along such a noble river as the
Irrawaddy. How the sight must have astonished
the natives, who crowded to the banks of the river
in great numbers as we passed, holding out poul-
try and vegetables to us; but we could not stop to
receive them, and our motion was too rapid to
enable their canoes to come alongside.

"The country has been free from jungle since

we left Panlang, but the banks of the river are covered with long thick reeds quite impenetrable. The regular Burmese have all left the country as ate advanced, and the Taylasin and Carian inhabitants are quite friendly, and hold free intercourse with us. But to return to our operations. On the 6th the whole fleet moved on early in the morning, and anchored opposite Donabew at noon. A number of boats and a party on shore went up the river about four o'clock to reconnoitre, when a heavy fire, evidently from large guns, was opened on them, and kept up with a quickness we had never before witnessed. The distance, however, was too great for them to do any execution, and the party returned without the loss of a man.

"At daylight on the 7th the troops landed: 100 of the 89th having been left on board, we mustered about 650 bayonets. We were formed into two columns; the right, composed of the 89th, led by Major Basden, advanced along the banks of the river to attack a stockade surrounding a large white pagoda; the left column, composed of the regiment, and part of H. M.'s 47th, under Colonel O'Donaugh, kept more to the left to attack the stockade at another point. Gwyn was the first man of our column who entered the stockade, and I had the good luck to be the first officer. The 89th were equally successful, and I think rather before us.

"A horrible slaughter took place, and 374 prisoners (most of them severely wounded,) and 230 dead bodies were actually counted, so that we had nearly a man to each musket. We also captured 3 guns, 43 jingalls with swords and spears innumerable, and a large quantity of ammunition. From the pagoda we had the first proper view of the enemy's position, which consisted of two stockades besides the one we had taken, extending nearly two miles along the banks of the river, the farthest and principal one completely commanding the second, or one nearest to our position at the pagoda.

"On the same day at about eleven o'clock, this last position was attacked by a party of 200 men from H. M, 89th, 47th, and Madras European regiment, commanded by Captain Rose; but after losing the Commanding Officer and Captain Cannon, and about 80 men killed and wounded, the party was obliged to retire. In consequence of this repulse, the troops were embarked during the night, without any interruption from the enemy. It was mortifying to us all to be obliged to do so, but from the drubbing we gave Bundoola in the morning, he had not much to boast of. On the following day dispatches were sent off to General Campbell for reinforcements, and we dropped down the river to the position we left on the 6th, where we have since remained until today. According to dispatches from General

Campbell, we expect him to join us tomorrow, and have in consequence again moved up to be in readiness, as it is probable the attack will be renewed immediately.

"17th—10 a. m. We have as yet received no further tidings of General Campbell, and as there is a signal now up for a packet being about to be dispatched, I have sat down to conclude. I expected to have done so in Donabew, and still hope to have the pleasure of telling you of its fall in a few days."

CHAPTER 18
Death of the Bundoola

On the 2nd April my friend writes again from Donabew:

"Donabew is at length ours, but we have been horribly tantalized and disappointed since we came before it. On the 17th ultimo, I gave you an account of our proceedings up to that date. It is now only two hours since we got into the place, and you may be sure that we are all bustle and confusion; but knowing that your thoughts are anxiously turned towards our operations, I have again sat down to devote a few minutes to bring you into the scene of action with us, being confident that you would prefer being here participating in our hardships and dangers, than in anything which is called enjoying luxury and comfort in the Carnatic. I have already told you that we have been disappointed. It has burned out nearly a second Kemmendine business. Our guns have taken the place eventually, and the infantry have had no opportunity of coming in contact with Bundoola and his picked men, in their own favourite position, rendered as strong as their ingenuity and persevering exertions could make it.

"General Campbell came up on the 26th; and the following day, Major Jackson came over to our position to communicate with us. He had a strong escort of 100 Europeans and 200 Natives; but on his return to the General's camp, he was intercepted by a strong party, who had made a sortie from the stockade, and obliged him to retreat to us: 200 Europeans from our division were landed to enable him to force his way back, but he declined their assistance, and came on board one of our brigs. On the following morning the steamer, with several row-boats in tow, carrying battering guns and ammunition, ran up the river and passed the stockade under a heavy fire, which nearly swamped one of the boats, as a ball entered just "between wind and water", and had the boatmen not rowed on shore with great expedition, many of the men on board must have been drowned, as they were all accoutred, but by good luck no further damage was done.

"Bundoola, we were told, had his most experienced artillerymen at the guns while the steamer was passing, who tried all they could to sink her; and so anxious was he himself on this point, that he assisted in pointing the guns, but without effect; he was so enraged at her passing uninjured, that he cut down several men at the guns. Next day a great number of war-boats were taken, and at night trenches were opened within 200 yards of the stockade.

"On the 28th batteries were commenced, and guns got into them on the night of the 29th. They were not, however, completed before the afternoon of the 1st, and at 8 o'clock the mortar and rocket battery opened and continued firing throughout the day, evidently doing execution. This morning the breaching battery opened, and a very heavy fire from it and the mortar battery was kept up for half an hour, but the enemy not returning it, the troops were turned out, and advanced to storm. We, however, walked in quietly, and to our astonishment found the place evacuated. Some wounded men who were taken prisoners reported that Bundoola was killed by a shell yesterday evening, which was a signal for the whole garrison to retreat. Had they stood, we must have sustained great loss, the defences of the place being incomparably stronger than any we have yet seen, and the garrison more numerous and better armed.

"However, strange as it may appear, I have felt less satisfaction upon finding ourselves master of it, than in gaining possession of the, smallest stockade which we have carried at the point of the bayonet on former occasions. The number of guns taken has not yet been correctly ascertained, but it is said two hundred guns, and three hundred jingalls have been counted, with an immense quantity of ammunition, and grain sufficient for the whole force for a twelvemonth.

"I have written this amidst a scene of uproar and confusion that will be an excuse for all blunders."

He writes again from Donabew:

"On the 8th I wrote you a hurried scrawl just after we got into the place, which, with our usual good luck, we have been left to garrison for the present, but Sir Archibald assured Conroy that it is only a temporary measure, and has promised to send for us before he quits Prome for Amerapoorah, and I trust he will adhere to his promise, as it is a great annoyance to us to be left here. But as they do not expect any opposition at Prome, it is of less consequence.

"The whole of the works here, including the white Pagoda, are upwards of six miles in circumference, I have not seen a return of the guns taken; but an artillery officer told me there were nearly three hundred, and about the same number of jingalls, with abundance of ammunition. There is also a large magazine well supplied with sulphur, saltpetre, lead, iron and other stores, a powder manufactory and arsenal, all within the large stockade. In the latter there were forty-odd forges and carpenters' shops, and an abundance of spears, gun-carriages, shot, swords, musket-stocks, etc., which they had been making up. In short they were well supplied with everything. Had not Bundoola fallen, we should have sustained a heavy loss before gaining possession of the place, the works were so extremely strong and the garrison so numerous, at least 15,000 men, all determined to conquer or fall with their leader, as they said; but the moment he fell, they became panic-struck, every one acted for himself: they quitted the stockade in confusion, and dispersed as soon as they reached the jungle.

"Bundoola was killed by a shell or rocket on the rampart opposite our breaching battery, where I picked up his jacket or gown, next morning, covered with blood, and a good deal torn. It is made of superfine white cloth, trimmed with green velvet, without any ornaments.

"General Campbell with the land force marched towards Prome on the 3rd, and General Cotton with the water party set off yesterday. They will enter the place about the 15th, and if expeditious, be able to reach Amerapoorah before the 1st of June.

"It has been stated that the regiment was left to garrison Donabew, but with a promise that we should be again called on to take an active share in the campaign as soon as the General could relieve us from that inglorious charge; and in September we embarked for Rangoon, previously to being sent to join the force under Colonel Pepper at Pegue, destined for the attack of Tonghoe.

CHAPTER 19

Settang Attacked

"We reached Pegue about the end of October, and by dint of the unceasing exertions of Colonel Pepper, sufficient carriage was secured from the inhabitants to enable us to leave our quarters by the 20th December, when the 3rd regiment N. I. was pushed forward to secure the means of transport at the village of Mekeed, on the banks of the Settang river, which they successfully accomplished.

"The river here was about a quarter of a mile broad at this season, but owing to its great depth, the rapidity of the current, and the slender means of transport at our disposal, two days elapsed before all the force, baggage, &c., were conveyed across. With the exception of the 3rd Light Infantry, commanded by Lieutenant Colonel Conroy, a chivalrous and enterprising officer, who were sent down the river in boats to drive the enemy from a stockade at Settang, said to have been hastily put into a state of defence, the remainder of the force moved on towards Shuaghien about thirty miles distant, in the direction of Tonghoe.

"The advanced guard was frequently fired on by the enemy, but there was no decided check to the steady advance of the column, until we approached within a few miles of Shuaghien, when a heavy fire was opened from a stockade at the verge of the jungle, which was screened from observation by an angle of the road, until we came quite close upon it. The guns were immediately unlimbered, and under a smart fire of grape-shot, three corps advanced to the attack in double time, and carried the work in good style, with but little opposition or loss, as the enemy fled before we could come to close quarters with them.

"The next day, on emerging from the jungle, we came in sight of the stockade of Shuaghien which looked, what we ultimately found it to be, a very formidable defence, being built of immensely thick beams of teak-wood, having small square bastions at intermediate distances, and was about twenty feet in height. Our nearer approach was checked by a branch of the river about seventy yards broad, that flowed between us and the stockade, which it became necessary to sound before we ventured to cross. It was however found to be quite fordable, and Captain Dickenson, the artillery officer, was ordered to unlimber and throw a few shells into the works previous to our attack, and as the fire was not returned by the enemy, we were directed to advance to the assault in three columns, and escalade—which was done; but to our mortification we found the stockade deserted.

"Here we remained for three days, and by the great exertions of Colonel Pepper, in sending out parties to scour the country, to prevent the Burmese from driving off the peaceable inhabitants of the district, we soon had the pleasure of seeing them return to their homes; and as the order issued by Colonel Pepper at the time will give a clear idea of the system pursued by the Burmese towards the inhabitants of the country, I shall insert it.

Shuaghien,

7th January, 1826

The duty entrusted to Captain Corbit, of pushing on his detachment to rescue the peaceable inhabitants of the surrounding country, about 1500 men, women and children, from a party of armed Burmese under a chief who was forcing them to Kongoo, has completely succeeded by the zealous exertions of that officer and his party: and it must be a pleasing gratification to them to know, that by their exertions so many people have been freed from the Burmese yoke, whose cruel and tyrannical conduct to them on the march was witnessed by the detachment, and, by their account, exceeds all bounds.

"It was during the time we remained at Shuaghien that a dispatch was received reporting the complete failure of the attack of the stockade at Settang by the 3d regiment Light Infantry, with the loss of Colonel Conroy and Lieutenant Adams, and many Sepoys, and a great number wounded, whilst endeavouring to carry the works by escalade. As this was a most serious check, and endangered the safety of our supplies and reinforcements at headquarters, and rendered the situation of the 3rd regiment at Mekew, to which place they had retired, very precarious, and also delayed our advance; the Colonel determined to give the enemy no time to glory in their victory, and therefore ordered the force at Shuaghien to hold itself in readiness to move the next morning.

"It is well known that Colonel Pepper detailed a portion of Europeans to act with Colonel Conroy's corps on this unpleasant occasion, but he, wishing to uphold the gallantry of the native troops, and particularly the Light Infantry battalions, requested as a favour that he might be allowed to lead his troops into action unsupported by Europeans. It was granted, and in consequence the Madras Army lost one of her best and bravest soldiers! On the following morning the flank companies of the regiment, a wing of the 12th regiment N. I. and two companies of the 34th regiment N. I. the whole commanded by Colonel Pepper, marched to Mekew, and there joined the 3rd regiment Light Infantry, when the force was embarked, and shortly after daylight the next morning we came in sight of the Settang stockade, which was seen from a considerable distance in consequence of the great height of the position on which the stockade is erected.

"At this time the tide began to turn, which rapidly filled all the little creeks, and somewhat scattered the boats of the flotilla. However, we landed in safety; but on examining our position, a narrow but deep creek was found to intercept our advance, running within two hundred yards of the foot of the hill on which the enemy's works were situated; and it was found impossible to cross until the tide began to ebb. The attack was therefore delayed until about three o'clock in the afternoon, when some of the tallest Grenadiers were placed in the middle of the stream to assist in passing the force over.

"It was a tedious work, but executed without accident, or damage to the ammunition, the pouches being slung on the tops of the muskets. Previous to fording the creek, it was arranged that the force should advance to the storm in three columns simultaneously at a given signal. Colonel Pepper conducted the left column, which consisted of the Grenadiers of the regiment, under Captain Carsham, and the 3rd Light Infantry. They had to make a considerable detour, and gradually ascended until they nearly attained the same elevation as the stockade, from whence they were to escalade. The centre column consisted of the light company of the regiment, under Lieutenant Howden; and two companies of the 34th Light

Infantry, commanded by Captain Steadman, were to storm the front face; the right columns composed of the 12th regiment N. I. were to be led to the attack by Captain Home of that regiment.

"I have omitted to mention that the dead bodies of Colonel Conroy, Lieutenant Adam, with the Sepoys, who fell on the former attack, were all found suspended to a cross-beam by the heels, naked, and horribly mutilated, which so exasperated our men, that they one and all declared they would have their revenge this day for such a barbarous act.

"Situated on a hill, the stockade held a most commanding position, and appeared to be well garrisoned, indeed we received intelligence of a strong reinforcement having entered the stockade since their late victory, and that, flushed with success, they were determined to defend their post to the last extremity. The stockade was quite impregnable on the river side, showing an almost perpendicular rocky acclivity of two hundred feet. The ascent in front of the centre column was also very steep, particularly within fifty paces of the summit, the ground leading to the gateway where the right column was ordered to attack was more gradual in its ascent.

"Before we advanced, it was impressed upon the European soldiers of the centre column, that should the pioneers carrying the ladders waver or be killed, they must immediately supply their places, and to this must principally be attributed its unchecked success.

"The advance was sounded on the concerted signal being given, when each column moved to the attack in column of sections, but the ascent was so steep and difficult, and the fire so heavy, that it was nearly a quarter of an hour before we reached the summit of the hill, where the footing was so narrow and bad, and the opposition so determined, that notwithstanding their utmost and repeated endeavours, the men at; the head of the column were unable to plant the ladders, when Lieutenant Chambers came up with the rear subdivision and another ladder, and by their united exertions they at length succeeded, when Lieutenant Chambers took the lead, and was the first who entered the stockade, rapidly followed by the whole column, when the enemy were routed in every direction, although fighting desperately to the last.

"In consequence of the left column having taken less care of their ladders, they were for a longer period under fire, as many of the pioneers who carried them were killed, when the Grenadiers were obliged to go back some fifty or sixty yards to bring them up; and it was on this occasion that that brave officer Captain Carsham received his death wound, at the head of the Grenadier company in the very act of escalading. Captain Steadman of the 34th Regiment was also killed;

Colonel Pepper, Captain Home, and Lieutenant Charlton were wounded, and two-thirds alone of our flank companies were either killed or wounded: indeed It was altogether a most gallant affair, and Colonel Pepper paraded the flank companies of the Regiment in the stockade of Settang, and thanked them personally for their perseverance and gallant bearing throughout the day.

Chapter 20

Peace

"After this, Colonel Pepper retraced his steps to Mekew, and finally to Shuaghien, where we were met by the remainder of the regiment who had not accompanied us to the attack of Settang, with the band of the regiment at their head, in readiness to escort us in honour to our old lines, which we were certainly not Prepared for, although we felt the honour truly, as it was intended.

"A few days subsequent we received intelligence of Peace being concluded. And thus ends the memoirs of the services of the regiment in Burmah, as the force retrograded to Pegue, and finally, in June, 1826, the regiment embarked for Masulipatam on board the transport *Argyle*."

I may well be allowed to say that the War in Burmah was distinguished by a course of personal suffering, and patient endurance, on the part of the army, almost without a parallel. On service a soldier grows familiar with privations, death and sorrow; but if he has an eve to observe, and a heart to feel, few men see or suffer more than a soldier.

A Brief History of the Army of the Honourable East India Company from the Beginning to 1857

G. F. MacMunn

Publisher's note: this short history of the army of the Honourable East India Company has been adapted by Leonaur's editors from *The Armies of India* by A. C. Lovett & G. F. MacMunn first published in 1911.

Introduction

The English have as yet ruled in India barely one-half the time that the Romans ruled in Britain, though their rule in the East has much in common with that of Rome north of the Channel. For the last century and a half have the English legions, European and Indian, tramped the trunk roads of Hindustan as those of Rome tramped Merry England before it was England at all up and down the length and breadth of India, as up and down Watling Street and the Via Fossa, or up and down "the legion's road to Rimini" at the legion's pace, have tramped those English legions since Clive decided that there should be one king and not a dozen in India, and that one, neither French nor Dutch nor Portuguese. And the marvel of it all is that these tramping disciplined legions are not the beef and porridge and potato-reared lads of the Isles, but for the most part men of the ancient races of Hindustan, ruled and trained and led after the manner of the English.

From the doorkeepers and trained bands that first guarded the factories of the early merchants, the army of John Company Bahadur grew and prospered, by the secret of ever-increasing scope and labour, till it became the great shako-clad army of the Line that vanished for the most part in the tragedy of '57. Of the three great presidential armies, the larger part, that of Bengal, and part of that of Bombay, disappeared, and with it the glorious record of successful war and faithful service, in a storm of unreasoned and uncalled-for mutiny, that buried in a month the tradition of a century. The army that now upholds the Empire of Hindustan, is based on a systematic grouping of men by race and sept and clan, with a view to the full development of race efficiency.

This careful grouping has been the subject of much attention during the last twenty years, and has called for a thorough study of the clans and tribal systems of India ending in a method of recruiting which is remarkable, and of a rank and file which is numerous and admirable. It is also well calculated to prevent the decline of martial qualities, which follows so quickly in the East on an era of peace. The results of twenty years of this system it is the object of this book to describe and illustrate. To arrive, however, at the present stage, and to understand that vast organization by class and clan which are illustrated herein, it is necessary to trace the rise of the armies of India through their separate presidential existence, to one vast whole.

CHAPTER 1

The Formation of an Army

The army of great John Company took its origin from three separate nuclei, separated by many miles of road and sea and hostile territory. These three centres originated in, first, "an ensign and thirty men", reinforced by a "gunner and his crew", stationed in Bengal towards the end of the seventeenth century; second, a detachment sent to garrison Bombay, the dower of Catherine of Braganza, Charles the Second's bride; and third, the forming of companies and soldiers from factory doorkeepers and watchmen in Madras. These curiously haphazard beginnings were the unmeditated foundations of three immense armies of horse, foot, and artillery.

The raising of actual native regiments was first undertaken by the French, and it was due to the coming struggle for mastery in Southern India that we owe the first conception of a regular native army. In 1748 Dupleix raised several battalions of Musalman soldiery armed in the European fashion in the Carnatic, and a few years later Stringer Lawrence followed suit in Madras, The distances that separated the three presidencies resulted in each force growing up on divergent principles and with different organizations, of which the ill results survive to some extent even to this day; European companies were formed from detachments sent from England, from runaway sailors, men of disbanded French corps, from Swiss and Hanoverians, from prisoners of war, and any white material in search of a livelihood. In 1748 the regular European corps of the Company's service, who now form part of the British Line and the Royal Artillery, were first formed from these heterogeneous detachments and scattered companies. In 1754 the first Royal troops came to take their share in garrisoning the East Indies, the 89th foot being the "first in the Indies". By 1759, two years after Plassey, six regular native battalions existed in Madras, and a few years later similar corps were formed in Bombay.

During the constant wars with the French, with Mysore and the Mahrattas, the presidential armies grew and developed and were brigaded. In 1793 the fall of Pondicherry for the last time ended once and for all the power of the French in India, though their influence lasted for many years after. When this great struggle came to an end, and Lord Cornwallis had humbled the Tiger of Mysore, and, after the manner of the English, given him one more chance, it became high time to put some organization and system into the mass of troops that had grown up during the years of war. So in 1795 we come upon the first general reconstruction, on a definite principle, throughout the three armies. At this date there were 13,000 Europeans in the country, King's and Company's, and some 24,000 native troops in Bengal and Madras respectively, with 9000 in Bombay. The reorganization took the accepted form of collecting artillery companies into battalions, cavalry troops into regiments, and forming the infantry into two-battalion regiments. This of course meant renumbering the whole of the battalions in each of the three armies except the first half, and incurring the usual dislike of corps for a change of the number under which they have won fame, however necessary that be. The uniforms of corps were more strictly assimilated to those of the King's troops, and a regular army came into being.

In those days the whole of India swarmed with men of military predilections. The Afghan races, who for the last sixty years have been cribbed and confined to their own hills, wandered at will through the land to sell their sword to the highest bidder. Every native chief had Arab and Afghan soldiery. Afghan soldiers of fortune, on the waning of the Mogul authority, had hacked their way to power and were forming principalities. The Rohillas, the descendants of Afghan and Turki settlers, still preserved many of their original characteristics, and drew fresh recruits from relatives in the border hills.

The old coast armies were largely filled by these adventurers or their half-bred children, or else by low-caste men, who on European food and with European leading gladly fought the high-caste races that had oppressed them. The irregular horse, which came into being in Lord Lake's time, was largely recruited from the soldiers of fortune and masterless men that broke away from the falling fortunes of the crumbling States. It should be remembered that in few cases were the rulers then going down before us more than mushroom kings—adventurers who had themselves displaced the old rulers or the old Mogul governors; in hardly any case had they more claim to power than "the good old rule; the simple plan". The slackening of the Mogul authority had been the signal for a vast scramble among the free-lances, in which the cruelty and oppression endured by the long-suffering peasantry was beyond belief. To every district from which British successes had driven the freelance and the alien Schwartweiter, the British uniform and the white face were a sign of freedom and mercy, when the peasant dare till the field and the woman creep out from her hovel

Then, too, because in every land, but more especially in the East, it is good to be on the winning side, soldiers of all kinds flocked to the Company's colours, and the leader of free-lances tried to preserve some *izzatl* in serving the new master, who at any rate paid regularly.

In 1798 Lord Mornington, later the Marquis Wellesley, became Governor-General, and, seeing farther ahead than most, realized that whatever the folk at home would say, the British in the East must either go forward or be overwhelmed, and that forthwith, and so determined that however so much others might care to fritter away an empire, he would have none of it. Already far-seeing men had settled that there was to be one European power in Hindustan, fighting the French wherever they found them, and Lord Mornington had determined that there should not only be one European power, but only one paramount power in the Peninsula. With the fall of the French State, French soldiers of fortune had drifted to most of the native courts of India, ready to minister to the desire for what then seemed the secret of power, troops trained on the European model. Mahratta and Musalman States, alarmed at the might of the English, were preparing to destroy the power of the Company. Buonaparte himself was openly trafficking with Tippoo in Mysore, with Scindia, with Holkar and the Bhonsla, the leading chiefs of the Mahratta confederacy, while the French Isles of France and Bourbon harboured privateers to prey on the Indiamen, and formed a base for designs on India itself.

So the great Marquis started forth himself to strike first, lest worse befall. Tippoo, the Tiger of Mysore, profiting little by the chance given him six years earlier by Lord Cornwallis, again broke a lance, and fell once and for all to General Harris. Arthur Wellesley and Stevenson broke the power of Scindia in two pitched battles and a dozen successful sieges and assaults. General Lake, the Commander-in-Chief, led his troops from Bengal against the chief gatherings of the Mahrattas, defeating Scindia's trained forces, the army that De Boigne and Perron had organized with such care, at Deig and Laswarrie. Delhi fell, the old blind Mogul was rescued from his Mahratta jailers and pensioned, and Holkar was chased by Lake for 350 miles, till he fled to his own country.

Then came the swing back of the pendulum, and the British took reverses that lessened their hold on the imagination of the East for many years to come. General Lake left the final pursuit of Holkar to a force under Colonel Monson of the 76th Foot, and that officer followed far away from his own base and into the season of the rains, until Holkar, tampering with his auxiliaries, and even with his regular troops, turned on him. Monson was compelled to retire, and the withdrawal gradually changed to a flight, and the flight to a debacle despite the heroism of his Europeans, and some of his native troops. The second reverse was the Commander-in-Chief's failure to take Bhurtpore, the capital of a Hindu State. Time after time were his columns, usually headed by the 76th Foot, hurled back from the impracticable breaches with heavy loss, till at last the old soldier reluctantly determined to abandon the siege of the great mud fortress; and for years after, when our action was thought high-handed, we were told to "go bully Bhurtpore". With the exception of these two failures, the three years' campaign against the Mahrattas was conspicuous by its success, and by the treaties which brought the States concerned, not within the actual British Empire, but to a definite state of allied feudatories, with in many cases their power for evil at any rate much curtailed.

During these wars more regiments, both horse and foot, were continually being raised, and after them the army became still more regular and controlled by regulation, in close touch with the increasing garrison of King's troops, and more and more European in its dress and equipment. Irregulars too were added to the army at this period, and as the question of regulars versus irregulars has been hotly argued in India in the past, it may be well to understand the difference. Today, the Silladar Cavalry are the legitimate heirs of the old irregulars, and the whole native army is largely modelled on what fifty years ago was termed the Irregular System. The regular army, both horse and foot, resembled in its organization the British Line. The establishment of officers resembled that of the King's service, and companies and troops were commanded by the British officers, while the native officers were but understudies promoted by seniority, and not for efficiency, and were men of great age. On the cross over the long trench graves on the battlefield of Chillianwalla are inscribed the names of two Brahman subadars, and against their names is recorded their ages, 65 and 70, In war time men no doubt came to commissioned rank earlier, but in peace under the regular system the native officers were aged figureheads. In the irregular corps the British officers were few, and native officers had definite command of companies and troops, and came to great authority and efficiency thereby. The irregular cavalry were enlisted on the old system of the country—the silladar system—whereby in return for a sum down the soldier came with horse, arms, and accoutrements complete. This is the system which, considerably developed, holds in the Indian cavalry today, with the exception of the three light cavalry regular regiments of the old Madras cavalry, which still exist as part of the old line, and which still wear the French grey and silver of the old regular light cavalry that played so leading a part in the Mutiny.

The irregulars were not esteemed at their worth by the rest of the army, till the wars in Afghanistan and the Punjab showed the immense value of the power of resource and initiative that they possessed. This was probably accentuated by the fact that while this spirit was far more present in all ranks in the earlier wars, the Pax Britannica had killed it among the peasantry and it only remained among a smaller class.

CHAPTER 2

Indian and Other Wars

It should be remembered that during the earlier years of the nineteenth century the Indian army fulfilled an essentially imperial role. The reduction of the overseas colonies and naval stations of our European enemies during the Napoleonic wars was entrusted to it. The overseas expeditions were numerous, and this power to commence expeditions from a self-supporting base, was and is one of the great strategical assets which India adds to our imperial power.

So early as 1762, an expedition composed of Madras troops took part in the war with Spain by capturing Manila. In 1795, an expedition from India captured Ceylon from the Dutch and French, the native troops being from Madras, with the exception of some artillery companies from Bengal. In 1795, an expedition from Madras captured Amboyna and the Spice Islands from the Dutch. In 1801, a force from India under Sir David Baird proceeded to join the British force in Egypt, the 2nd and 13th Bombay Infantry and some native artillery taking part. In 1808, a force of volunteers from the Bengal army proceeded to occupy Macao with a view to forestalling the French.

In 1810, the depredations of the French privateers on

British commerce demanded the capture of Mauritius, Bourbon and Rodrigues. Expeditions, in which Bombay and Madras corps and volunteer battalions from the Bengal army took part, reduced the islands with little difficulty. In 1811, a large naval and military force proceeded to capture the Island of Java from the Dutch and French. The troops included several volunteer battalions from Bengal, and some horse artillery and pioneers from Madras, The expedition met with considerable resistance, and was entirely successful.

The end of the Mahratta Wars of 1803-4 meant no prolonged peace for the Indian Army. In 1814 broke out the war with Nepal due to Gurkha inroads, and after preliminary disasters was brought to a successful conclusion when General Ochterlony took the field with fresh troops and selected generals. From this time, after the manner of the English, the conquered race was formed into soldiers, and from it spring the Gurkha battalions that are such a famous part of the Indian Army of today.

In 1817 there were two causes that once more involved India in a far-reaching war. The Mahratta States, chafing under treaties, and garrisons that prevented their overrunning the territories of their weaker neighbours, were busy planning fresh resistance, while allied with them and even a worse evil, were the Pindaris. This was the name given to the enormous bands of free-lances, who, seizing strongholds and forming centres wherever they pleased, scourged the country round, swept and raided where they wished, and brought half India to the state of Europe in the days of Wallenstein and Tilly. These vast bodies of masterless soldiery, chiefly horse with many odd guns, had grown from the gradual break-up of Mogul armies, and had continually been reinforced from Afghan tribesmen, Arabs, and any adventurous and lawless lad who liked to hear the lark sing rather than the mouse squeak, and they lived at their ease on the peasantry of India.

In 1817, therefore, things had come to such a pass, that if we were to keep India as a land for honest men to live in, the Mahratta confederacy must be reduced to a proper status, and the Pindaris driven from the land. If we realize the Pindaris were operating over a country about twice the size of France, and provided by nature with every kind of bolthole and fastness, we shall perhaps understand the task that Lord Moira, the Governor-General, had set himself. The combined forces of the Mahratta States and the Pindaris amounted to at least 100,000 horse, 70,000 disciplined foot, and over 500 guns. Against these, the Indian Army took the field in two large forces—the Army of the Deccan, commanded by Sir Thomas Hislop, consisting of seven divisions, and the Grand Army, commanded by the Governor-General himself, consisting of four divisions. Both armies were strong in cavalry, there being several regiments of Rohilla horse, with Gardner's and Skinner's Irregulars, and most of the regular native cavalry, as well as several regiments of British light dragoons, which were reduced in subsequent intervals of peace.

The events of this campaign are too numerous to be described in detail, but among the most famous are the defence of Seetabuldee (the Nagpore Residency), the battles of Kirkee against the Peshwa, the battle of Mahidpore against Holkar, and the famous battle of Corygaum near Poona, where the 2nd/1st Bombay Infantry, with 250 horse and a detachment of Madras Artillery, resisted the most desperate attacks of the whole of the Peshwa's army. When the main forces opposing us had been crushed as an army in being, many weary months followed in chasing Mahratta and Pindari bands from one stronghold to another, and reducing innumerable hill forts, till the land had peace. Perhaps the feature of this war was the increasing number of irregular horse, who proved far the best suited to the final stage of the work, and the subsequent attempt to improve the organization of the army, that had shown defects in the wide strain put on it.

It must not be supposed that in all these years of an alien army there had not been mutinies; a large army controlled by a trading company, with large ideas on the subject of profits, was bound to have passed through periods of well-founded grievance. In 1806 had been the serious mutiny of Vellore—that should have been as the writing on the wall—and in 1824 the corps ordered to march to Arracan had refused to go. In 1824 the whole of the armies were reorganized and renumbered, the double-battalion regiments being abolished, and the line in each army was renumbered from *one* upwards by single battalions, receiving their new numbers in accordance with their original date of formation.

From the close of the Pindari wars, the expedition to Burma in 1824, and the capture of Bhurtpore, were the chief military events till we come to the First Afghan War. It will be remembered how, in 1803, Lord Lake was compelled to attend on the siege of Bhurtpore after losing 446 killed and 2479 wounded, in four separate assaults. In 1825 the insolence of the rulers of this virgin fortress knew no bounds, and circumstances forced the Government to reduce it. The Commander-in-Chief, Lord Combermere, advanced against the place in December 1825, with a force consisting of a cavalry and two strong infantry divisions, backed up, by what Lord Lake so lacked, half the heavy guns in India. The fortress was eventually stormed, with the loss of close on 1000 killed and wounded, and a loss to the garrison computed at 8000. The prestige thus regained by the British was great.

For twelve years after the fall of Bhurtpore the army had comparative peace. As a result of the Marquis Wellesley's policy, and that followed by the Marquis of Hastings (Lord Moira) after the close of the Pindari war, there grew up many contingents paid for by the native States, but commanded by Company's officers, drilled like our own troops, and enlisting, in the case of the majority, the same races as the Bengal Army. Service in some of them was much sought after, and the Gwalior contingent came to be regarded as a *corps d'elite* famed for its discipline and appearance.

In 1838 a policy was adopted which was to involve India in four years' war, immense disaster and chagrin, and a loss of prestige to which perhaps the Mutiny is of all causes most directly traceable. This policy consisted of forming a friendly Afghanistan to assist in opposing the advance of the Bear. The rightful ruler of Afghanistan, Shah Soojah ul Mulk, driven forth by his own folk by reason of his incompetence, was a pensioner in our midst. He had apparently sufficient following to justify our restoring him as our ally, should that course seem desirable, which to the brains of the time it did. There was no question of right or wrong.

On all and every occasion Afghans had swept into Hindustan to slay, to rape, to loot, and to devastate. If, in the policy of security and good government, it was desirable to turn the tables, it was only a question of expediency and counting the cost, and the pros and cons. At any rate, to those in power the course seemed good, and the famous "Tripartite Treaty" was signed between ourselves, the Shah, and Ranjit Singh, the Maharaja of the Punjab. To place His Highness on the throne of his fathers and maintain him there, a contingent was raised in India, with British officers, of Hindustanis and Gurkhas and to support it the Army of the Indus was collected. Since, however, the Punjab was foreign, and not too trustworthy, it was decided to advance into Afghanistan by the lengthy if easier route of Sukkur, Quetta, Kandahar, and Ghussnee. The force consisted of a brigade of cavalry, a Bengal division, a Bombay column, and the Shah's contingent, 6000 strong. The force under Sir John Keane reached Kabul in 1839, after the successful storming of Ghuznee, and immense trouble due to want of carriage, cold and sickness, and after abandoning the useless baggage and camp followers responsible for much of the trouble. All was *couleur de rose*. The Shah sat on the throne of his fathers; much of the army was withdrawn; English officers rode freely over the country; the Khyber route was opened; ladies, children, soldiers, families, flocked to the cantonment at Kabul; the contingent garrisoned the outposts, the brigades of occupation sat in Kabul and Kandahar. All was peace and content on the surface.

Then came the sinister rumours, the gathering of the storm, the murder of the Envoy Sir William Macnaghten and the Envoy-elect Sir Alexander Burnes, the squabbles of an effete commander and inefficient garrison, the attempt to evacuate Kabul in the snow, the taking of hostages, and lastly, the massacre of half-frozen troops and frost-bitten followers—such a disaster and humiliation as had never before happened to British arms. Bright spots there were. The defence of Kelat-i-Ghilzai by the 3rd Shah's, now the 12th (Kelat-i-Ghilzai) Regiment, under Captain Craigie, with a few European artillerymen, the defence of Jellalabad by Sale and the "Illustrious garrison", the sturdy demeanour of Nott at Kandahar, with his "splendid Sepoy regiments", all were bright spots, to redeem incompetence and pusillanimity. But the world looked at the failure; a British brigade annihilated under most pitiable circumstances was what the Eastern world saw, and rejoiced at. Then came the avenging army under Pollock, with trembling sepoys to be heartened and redisciplined at Peshawar, and a final advance, not so much to rescue the English men and women in captivity as to help the sturdy Nott, who had agreed with Pollock to carry out the orders to evacuate Afghanistan by coming via Kabul on their joint responsibility. This method of evacuating Afghanistan enabled vengeance to be taken on the guilty capital, and the British prisoners to be rescued.

The armies of Nott and Pollock then marched down

from Kabul, and after traversing an almost hostile Punjab, passed the British frontier into Ferozepore, to find an immense reception awaiting them from the Governor-General, Lord Ellenborough, at the head of a reserve army. An interesting incident of the times, was the intense camaraderie between the 13th Foot and the 35th Bengal Native Infantry, parts of the "Illustrious garrison", which ended in the whole of the latter feasting their British comrades before parting at Ferozepore. Even the 35th, however, went under in '57, and with them the battery of artillery on whose guns Lord Ellenborough had engraved a mural crown for its share in the defence. Despite, however, the triumphant finale, the maimed and frost-bitten remnants of the earlier occupation, rescued from begging in the Kabul bazaars, told a tale of lessened prestige that was not forgotten for many years.

During the strain of the Afghan War, however, India was still able to find troops for Imperial overseas purposes. In 1840, a large amount of British property had been destroyed by the Chinese in an attempt to solve by a short cut the opium problem, and an expedition under Sir Hugh Gough was sent to South China. The major portion of the force were troops of the Madras Line, for, as it had become a habit for the Bengal Army not to cross the seas, the usual volunteer battalions alone represented the Bengal Army. An aftermath of the Afghan wars was the trouble in Scinde, ending in Sir Charles Napier's short and famous campaign, in which three Bombay Cavalry, a Regiment of Bengal Native and two Bombay Infantry regiments took part with the 22nd Foot. The annexation of Scinde that followed, still further extended the responsibilities of the sepoy army, and necessitated more battalions.

This same year, 1843, was to see an important though short campaign in internal India, A minority in Scindia's domain, the State of Gwalior, had resulted in dissensions between two factions.

The army took opposite sides to that supported by Government, and the army was a very considerable force, still retaining the European organization and drill that it had learnt in the days of De Boigne and his successors. Gwalior was a large Hindu State, and there was considerable danger of an attempt to combine with the other great Hindu power, the Sikhs of the Punjab. To obviate any outbreak of the Gwalior troops, an army of exercise was collected as a precautionary measure near Agra, and another force at Jhansi. Eventually the state of affairs at Gwalior necessitated a move of the British troops on the capital, but it was not expected to be more than a promenade, and some ladies even accompanied the force. While Sir Hugh Gough advanced from Muttra, Sir John Grey advanced from Jhansi, and to every one's surprise, the Mahratta army was found in position near Maharajpore, and also at Punniar. The former force opened fire on Sir Hugh Gough, and a severe engagement ensued, in which the Gwalior artillery was especially well served. The battle at Punniar was also a severe one, though on a lesser scale. These two victories, however, completed the overthrow of the Gwalior troops and ended the disturbing conditions in the Durban.

CHAPTER 3

The End of an Era

In the winter of 1845 the most serious trouble that had threatened India for many years came to a head. The Sikhs, who had lost the firm hand of the sagacious Ranjit Singh, and were burning to invade British India, finally crossed the Sutlej in large numbers near Ferozepore. The native troops that took part in the campaign were entirely from Bengal, and acquitted themselves with varying credit. The Sikhs were far the severest foe that had been met in India, and the climate was rigorous to natives of Hindustan, while there was considerable feeling towards the last Hindu State. The bulk of the fighting fell on the European troops, whose casualties were very severe.

Large additions were made to the army at the outbreak of the campaign, including the formation of eight more regiments of cavalry. The cantoning of a force of occupation at Lahore during the minority of the young Maharaja, put some strain on the army, and a special force was raised for the garrisoning of the Jullundur Doab.

The attempt to bolster up the Sikh State, that was adopted as a definite policy after the First Sikh War, was soon doomed to failure. The Sikhs had not yet made up their minds to accept even British domination, and an outburst was precipitated by the murder, at Mooltan, of two British officers lent to the Durbar. This took place in the early summer of 1848, and it was some time before a force for the reduction of Mooltan, into which Mool Itaj, the rebellious Sikh governor, had thrown himself, could be assembled. Events, too, soon showed that the outbreak at Mooltan was likely to become general, and a large army was organized at Ferozepore, consisting of four brigades of cavalry and three divisions of infantry.

The reinforcement of the force attacking Mooltan, by a Bombay brigade, the final capture of the fortress, the passing of the Chenab, the hard-fought battle of Chillianwalia, the final crushing of the Sikhs at Gujarat, and the surrender of the Sirdars and their followers at Rawalpindi, with the pursuit of the Afghan horse to the Khyber, are all matters of history and of full record.

Suffice it here to say that the Bengal native army formed the bulk of the force, reinforced for the crowning victory of Gujarat by the Bombay brigade that had taken part in the storm of Mooltan. The brunt of the heavy fighting in this war fell as usual on the European troops, but some of the native infantry corps were especially distinguished and suffered very heavy casualties. The losses sustained by the British troops in these two Sikh wars were very severe, far more so than any portion, especially the native infantry, had been accustomed to experience for many years.

The annexation of the Punjab was followed by more additions to the native army, with very little corresponding increase in the European garrison, while the exigencies of holding the immense area annexed, and of watching the Afghan frontier demanded a grouping of the European troops in the North of India, and a very large native garrison. The frontier brigade organized in the Juhundtir Doab was moved to the Afghan border, and from it, with the addition of several new corps, recruited largely from the Khalsa regiments that had been disbanded, the Punjab irregular Force was formed. Lord Dalhousie's policy of annexing States in hopeless anarchy, or which had no successor in heredity on the demise of the reigning chief, added considerably to the demands on the native force in the country.

In 1854 the annexation of Nagpore necessitated the formation of local force, and the annexation of Oudh in 1856 was perforce followed by the immediate formation of the Oudh Irregular Force. It should be realized that the state of the country, with its poor communications and immense hilly and jungle tracts, demanded far more effective forces than police, for the ordinary pacification and maintenance of order in the districts. In countries where might had been right for perhaps a couple of hundred years, and the hand alone had kept the head since the memory of man, there were scores of reiving barons and robber chiefs to be dealt with. To make the barons and their retainers pay revenue, obey the law, and cease to spoil the peasant and the trader, was for many years beyond the power of mere police, and it was this need, coupled with the fact that revenue was by no means ample, that demanded troops, and those of the cheaper, or native, kind. The policy, therefore, dangerous though it seemed, was an almost unavoidable one, given the conditions as they appeared to men at the time.

The war in the Crimea had withdrawn some European troops from India which had not been replaced in 1857. The Second Burmese War, unavoidably thrust on us in 1853, had called for still more troops of occupation, and in 1856, a Persian expedition removed several European corps for the time beyond the seas. Several native corps of the Bombay Army took part in the Persian expedition and gained considerable distinction. Between 1849 and 1857 the new frontier at the foot of the Afghan hills gave much trouble, and numerous small frontier expeditions, to impress the laws of *meum* and *teum* on the tribes, were necessary.

The foregoing in brief is the outline of the causes which gradually formed the huge Indian Army, and of the magnitude and the vastness of the services it rendered both in India and in the Empire generally. Minor infidelities and mutinies there had been and many failings of the service as a whole had been often pointed out, with many aberrations of judgment on the part of the administration. The fact remains, however, that come rain come shine, this vast alien force had, for a hundred and fifty years, rendered the most faithful military service to their masters, while an immense feeling of attachment had grown up among officers and men.

On the March
to Chitral

By George Pridmore
Bedfordshire Regiment

Taken from the Leonaur book
Tommy Atkins' War Stories

On the March
to Chitral

I went out to India with my regiment in 1891, and first heard about the Chitral Expedition on St. Patrick's Day, 17th March 1895.

It was Sunday morning, and we were on church parade at Peshawar when the news came, and we were told to be ready to march in twenty-four hours' time. Up till then we had heard nothing of the terrible danger which threatened the British agent, Surgeon-Major Robertson, and his gallant little band of native soldiers, in the besieged fort at Chitral. We had only heard a vague rumour that war was in the air.

The next twenty-four hours were pretty busy, I can assure you, for an enormous quantity of arrangements have to be made for a campaign in a wild country, cut off by high mountains from any centre of civilisation, but, of course, the burden of making these arrangements fell most heavily upon the officers.

We were ready in time, though no less than twenty-eight thousand pack animals -- mules and camels -- had to be collected to convey the baggage and food. You must remember that when war is carried on in a civilised country it is easy to buy or seize provisions on the road, but

ON THE MARCH TO CHITRAL

between Peshawar and Chitral the country consists of desolate mountains and wild valleys, with only small native villages at long intervals. It was necessary, therefore, to carry everything with us, yet matters were so well arranged that our baggage only amounted to ten pounds for each man and forty pounds for each officer.

For some reason our departure was delayed, and we remained under canvas till the 28th, when we started on a two days' march to Nowsbera, which was made the base of operations. On the following day we removed to Mardan, an eighteen miles' march. At least, it was officially called eighteen miles, but it really was a good deal more. Here the three brigades concentrated. The first, to which I belonged, consisted of the Bedfordshire Regiment, the 60th Rifles, the 15th Sikhs, and the 37th Dogras.

The march, which occupied six hours, was fearfully fatiguing. The sun was blazing hot, and the road was very dusty. Each of us carried his overcoat and a hundred rounds of ammunition, so that we were glad to buy lemonade from the natives whenever there was a chance. General Kinloch was in command of our brigade; General Sir Robert Low having command of the entire expedition. At Mardan we bivouacked for the night, each man lying out on the open ground.

The following morning we went on to Lundkwar, where we remained until the next day. The march was a very wearisome one, over hilly country where there was often no road. Sometimes we were following native tracks, at others crossing fields, and then again scrambling over rocks. As we carried no tents on this expedition (in order to reduce the baggage as much as possible), we had again to bivouac for the night.

This is unpleasant at the best of times in a tropical country. Not only are the nights very chilly, but the creeping things are simply legion. First there are the ants, which march over you in armies, and often get inside your clothes and bite desperately. Some species in particular seem to bite you with red-hot teeth. Then there are scorpions and centipedes, which sting and bite in a far worse fashion. I have known men suffer very severely for hours after being attacked by them. Of course, when you are lying out on the open ground at night, you are in constant danger from these creatures.

Wild beasts never come near the camp, except the jackals, which are not at all dangerous, though they are most shocking thieves. The man who has drawn his rations over night will probably find nothing but the smell left in the morning.

The night we spent at Lundkwar was more than usually trying, for it rained heavily, and we got quite wet through. Each of us had two blankets and a waterproof sheet. The latter is supposed to be used to keep us off the damp ground, but it is a common practice for two or three men to club together and construct a sort of gipsy tent with the aid of their sheets and some sticks. But when we lay down, the weather was fine, so that we took no precautions. In the morning you could see men everywhere sitting wrapped in blankets, with their clothes spread out to dry, and under these circumstances the British army did not present a very imposing spectacle.

In the morning we were hindered by the weather, and although the "Reveille" sounded at four o'clock it was nine before we set out for Shahkot, near the Malakhand Pass, which we were to storm.

There are three ways by which it is possible to cross the mountains which form the boundary of India at this point, and so to gain entrance to the Swat Valley, which lies on the road to Chitral. These are the Mora Pass, the Shahkot Pass, and the Malakhand Pass. Each of them is about three thousand five hundred feet high, and the path is about as rough as it well could be.

The General in command heard that all three passes were strongly held by hostile Swats, and he decided that the Malakhand Pass should be attacked. So he had ordered us to bivouac at Lundkwar, which is near the Shahkot Pass, in order to make the natives think that we were going to attack it, while a body of cavalry rode up to the Mora Pass to alarm the natives in that quarter. By this means he prevented the enemy from concentrating their forces on the Malakhand, which was the real point of attack.

It was on April 3rd that the battle, was fought, the very day -- as we afterwards heard -- when Colonel Kelly and his gallant little band of natives crossed the Shandhur Pass, far away to the north, struggling through five feet of snow, and actually carrying the cannon on their backs. Our 2nd Brigade led the attack under General Waterfield, the 1st Brigade acted as support, and the 3rd was held in reserve.

The Swats were about twelve thousand in number, about half of them being armed, and were spread over a mile and a half. They were stationed on the heights on either side of the pass, and had their *sangars* -- small breastworks of stone behind which to crouch and shoot -- ranged on all the spurs. Those who were not armed occupied themselves in rolling great stones down the steep mountain-side as our men rushed up to the attack. Our officers said that the position was such a strong one that a well-disciplined force might have held it for a week. As things were, it was captured after five hours' fighting.

First of all, the Guides and the 4th Sikhs were sent to climb the heights on the right, and then to attack the enemy's flank while the main charge was made in front. But so steep and rough was the climbing that they did not reach the top until the pass was practically won. In the meantime our three batteries were brought into action, and one by one the *sangars* on the hillsides were carefully shelled. Then the King's Own Scottish Borderers and the Gordon Highlanders advanced to the attack. They made a splendid dash up an almost perpendicular slope of more than a thousand feet, in the teeth of a perfect avalanche of stones, which the Swats were busily rolling down upon them.

Next the 1st Brigade set out, the 60th Rifles and the 15th Sikhs attacking in front, while the Bedfordshire and the 37th Dogras made for the enemy's left.

In this way the whole line got up near the pass. A short pause was made for the stragglers to get into position, and then bayonets were fixed and the "Charge" sounded. The three regiments then made a united dash for the crest, and with a great shout the position was carried at the point of the bayonet, and the pass was stormed.

The Swats fled in all directions, like chaff before the wind, and the Bedfordshire Regiment and the 37th Dogras pursued them down the farther valley till they reached the village of Khar, on the Swat River.

During the engagement about five hundred of the natives were killed, and nearly a thousand wounded; while we had less than seventy killed and wounded. The reason our loss was so small was just this. The Swat races are very poor marksmen. Their usual method is to sight their weapons for a certain mark beforehand, and they keep firing at this throughout the battle. If any of our men got within the line of fire they would probably be hit, but our method was first to send a few men forward to make a dust and induce the enemy to fire. Then we noticed where the bullets hit, kept just outside the mark, and picked off our opponents. In this way most of the enemy's fire proved a simple waste of powder and shot.

I was on convoy duty, much to my disappointment, so that I took no active part in storming the Malakhand Pass, but I had a fine view of the engagement. For five hours the Swats faced a most deadly fire without flinching, although we used mountain batteries, and they were largely armed with old flintlocks, and in some cases had to actually apply lighted matches to their rifles to make them go off. It is true that a certain number of them were armed with Martini-Henris and Sniders, but they could not use them to much effect.

How did they get these? Well, most of them were probably stolen from our troops in North India. These hill tribes are most expert thieves. They enter the camp at night without a sound, and, if any bungalow door has been left unlocked, something will be sure to have vanished before morning. I have known many a man to lose his rifle in this way. The thieves come naked and well oiled, so that if caught they nearly always wriggle out of our clutches and escape.

But they were wonderfully plucky in the fight. After the battle a good number of wounded natives came into camp for treatment, for I suppose you know that it is the custom in the British army to render full medical assistance to any wounded foes who care to avail themselves of it. Well, the number of wounds that some of these men carried was simply astonishing. One man had six bullets through him, and then walked nine miles to a village, where he was treated by one of our army surgeons, and actually recovered!

One man stood on the top of a hut and beat a tom-tom to encourage his comrades. Several times he dropped wounded, but each time struggled up again, until at last he was shot through the heart and fell headlong down the cliff. One of their standard-bearers was knocked over by our bullets again and again before he was finally killed.

One incident which occurred during the fight was especially remarkable. We noticed a man standing on a high peak with a signalling-flag. He had evidently belonged to some of our native troops, for he was an expert signaller, and as he watched our operations with the batteries -- which were now aimed at the sangars -- he signalled the result of each shot for the benefit of his comrades. Thus we saw him making the usual signals for "too high," "too low," "on the right," and so on, as the case might be. Of course that sort of thing was not convenient, so we sent a shell where we thought it would do most good, and blew the signaller all to pieces. The moment he was hit, another native sprang to the spot, caught up the flag, and signalled a bull's eye!

When the fight was over, the half-company, who had pursued the retreating Swats to Khar, camped for the night in the village. They had no food with them, but the natives, seeing who were the winning party, soon came with great professions of friendship and gave them rice and fruit, as well as straw for bedding and wood for fires. For a wonder the food was not poisoned, and our men spent a quiet night. In the meantime one company stayed in the pass for the night, and the rest of us bivouacked below it. Each man had a ration of biscuits, bully-beef, and rum.

About midnight we were called up and received orders to start at once and cross the pass in the dark. This was a most difficult business, as we had to get all our baggage along a narrow Buddhist road, which was nothing more than a rough footpath up the mountainside, and in many places was extremely steep. Halfway up we met a company of troops coming down for more baggage, and the result was that -- what with the crowding and the darkness -- we got hopelessly blocked for two hours, and did not reach the pass until eight o'clock in the morning. Here we had our breakfast of chupatties, rice, and tea, and then waited while the rest of the convoy struggled up the mountain.

It was a tremendous business to drag and push our

heavy ammunition baggage over the pass. A lot of us were told off to improve the Buddhist road, which was said to be two thousand years old, and when we had cleared away the stones and filled up the holes, the work was not quite so difficult. But, it was still quite hard enough. We carried our bedding in great bundles strapped to the sides of the mules, our boots and coats being put inside the bedding. Every now and then we would come to a narrow place between two rocks, where the mule stuck fast. Under these circumstances he generally fell down and refused to move till we had unloaded him, and then he would roll and kick and struggle, while the whole company was brought to a standstill. There is no creature on earth so wicked as a mule—except a camel!

My company, which went across in the dark, lost forty-three coats and bedding, besides a large number of boots. Many a man found himself with only one boot next day. But most of these things were found and brought along by the rear guard.

About one o'clock the whole column moved down to the Swat Valley, which we reached at three o'clock.

While we were on the march, the 1st Brigade had gone on ahead into the valley and was attacked by thousands of Swats, who came rushing from the Shahkot and Mora Passes when they found that the Malakhand had been taken. We could see them in the plains in front, and on the spurs of the hills to the right, waving flags, and evidently in a state of great excitement. The 37th Dogras and the Mountain Artillery were sent forward to hold them in check until we had got all our baggage clear of the pass.

Towards evening, as we made no attack upon them, the enemy became bolder, and were evidently contemplating an open attack upon us. Accordingly the few cavalry men who had now crossed the pass were ordered to advance round the spur which concealed us from the Swats, and to watch for an opportunity of driving them back. This body of cavalry consisted of only fifty sabers of the Guides under Captain Adams, who, with remarkable pluck and daring, at once charged the enemy and drove the whole of them back into the mountains.

There were at this time about two thousand Swats in the open, and the fact that fifty horsemen were able to drive them back had a most terrifying effect upon them. The prompt success of this little party of Guides was no doubt largely due to the fact that horse soldiers were quite unknown in the country, and the natives had no idea that we could get them across the pass. That so small a band was bold enough to charge forty times their own number must have taken their breath away. At any rate the natives completely lost heart, and next morning they had disappeared from the neighbourhood. We only lost seven or eight of our men, but at least two hundred and fifty of the Swats were killed.

Some of the natives showed great spirit on this occasion, before the cavalry appeared on the scene. A few of them actually rushed upon the Dogras, and cut a man down before they could be driven off. While the fighting was going on we were entertained with the music of several stolen bugles, which the Swats evidently thought would assist them in gaining the victory!

When all had got quiet, we bivouacked in square for the night, with our baggage and mules inside.

As part of the bedding was still on the other side of the pass, we had a pretty uncomfortable time as we lay there in the open. Every man was fully dressed and armed, and we kept in square, as there was the probability that the Swats might try to attack us under cover of the darkness. But they had been too thoroughly scared, and the night passed quite quietly.

The next day all the rest of our baggage was brought over the pass, and then we made a reconnaissance towards Thana, where the enemy could be seen in large numbers. After this the 1st Brigade, to which I belonged, stayed at Khar to guard the Swat Valley, and great was our disappointment to find that we were not to share the perils and the glory of the 2nd and 3rd Brigades, which at once pushed forward towards Chitral.

On the 6th of April the main body prepared to cross the Swat River. About four thousand five hundred of the enemy were massed upon the low hills which come right down to the northern bank of the river, and were reinforced by a number of riflemen sent down by the rebel chief, Umra Khan, under command of his brother.

Now it was evident that to cross the river in the teeth of such a force would mean the loss of a large number of our men, so General Waterfield arranged a clever stratagem. While we harassed the enemy with our batteries from the south side of the river, the Guides Cavalry and the 11th Bengal Lancers went a long way up the river, crossed by a ford, and fell upon the flank and rear of the enemy.

This proved a most effective plan, for no sooner did the Swats see the dreaded horsemen dashing down upon them than they completely lost heart and were soon in full flight.

Preparations were at once made for crossing the river with the aid of inflated skins. This was a dangerous business, as the river was at that season a rushing torrent, and the men were up to their armpits. Two or three were washed away and drowned.

After this the main force moved on, and we saw no more of them. On the 13th a sharp fight took place on the banks of the Panjkora River, and on the 17th Umra Khan was defeated at Munda, and fled from the country, thus virtually ending the campaign.

It was on the following night that the besieged garrison at Chitral was relieved by the little band of Sikhs who formed Kelly's relief force, and who had accomplished one of the most remarkable marches on record. But no British soldiers fought at Chitral, and, with the exception of a very small advance guard, none of our men ever went so far.

We who were left behind at Khar stayed there till May 25th, and then went to a hill station at Laram Khotam for the hot season. There remained till August 14th, when we returned to Rawal Pindi, and were once more on British territory.

LEONAUR
ALSO FROM LEONAUR
AVAILABLE IN SOFTCOVER OR HARDCOVER WITH DUST JACKET

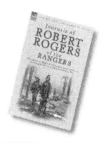

LEONAUR
ALSO FROM LEONAUR
AVAILABLE IN SOFTCOVER OR HARDCOVER WITH DUST JACKET

RGW1 RECOLLECTIONS OF THE GREAT WAR 1914 - 18
STEEL CHARIOTS IN THE DESERT *by S. C. Rolls*

The first world war experiences of a Rolls Royce armoured car driver with the Duke of Westminster in Libya and in Arabia with T.E. Lawrence.

SOFTCOVER : **ISBN 1-84677-005-X**
HARDCOVER : **ISBN 1-84677-019-X**

RGW2 RECOLLECTIONS OF THE GREAT WAR 1914 - 18
WITH THE IMPERIAL CAMEL CORPS IN THE GREAT WAR *by Geoffrey Inchbald*

The story of a serving officer with the British 2nd battalion against the Senussi and during the Palestine campaign.

SOFTCOVER : **ISBN 1-84677-007-6**
HARDCOVER : **ISBN 1-84677-012-2**

EW3 EYEWITNESS TO WAR SERIES
THE KHAKEE RESSALAH
by Robert Henry Wallace Dunlop

Service & adventure with the Meerut Volunteer Horse During the Indian Mutiny 1857-1858.

SOFTCOVER : **ISBN 1-84677-009-2**
HARDCOVER : **ISBN 1-84677-017-3**

WF1 THE WARFARE FICTION SERIES
NAPOLEONIC WAR STORIES
by Sir Arthur Quiller-Couch

Tales of soldiers, spies, battles & Sieges from the Peninsular & Waterloo campaigns

SOFTCOVER : **ISBN 1-84677-003-3**
HARDCOVER : **ISBN 1-84677-014-9**

LEONAUR

ALSO FROM LEONAUR

AVAILABLE IN SOFTCOVER OR HARDCOVER WITH DUST JACKET

EYEWITNESS TO WAR SERIES

CAPTAIN OF THE 95th (Rifles) *by Jonathan Leach*—An officer of Wellington's Sharpshooters during the Peninsular, South of France and Waterloo Campaigns of the Napoleonic Wars.

RIFLEMAN COSTELLO *by Edward Costello*—The adventures of a soldier of the 95th (Rifles) in the Peninsular & Waterloo Campaigns of the Napoleonic wars.

THE KHAKEE RESSALAH *by Robert Henry Wallace Dunlop*—Service & adventure with the Meerut volunteer horse during the Indian mutiny 1857-1858

BUGLER AND OFFICER OF THE RIFLES *by William Green & Harry Smith* With the 95th (Rifles) during the Peninsular & Waterloo Campaigns of the Napoleonic Wars

BAYONETS, BUGLES AND BONNETS *by James 'Thomas' Todd*—Experiences of hard soldiering with the 71st Foot - the Highland Light Infantry - through many battles of the Napoleonic wars including the Peninsular & Waterloo Campaigns

A NORFOLK SOLDIER IN THE FIRST SIKH WAR *by J W Baldwin*—Experiences of a private of H.M. 9th Regiment of Foot in the battles for the Punjab, India 1845-46

A CAVALRY OFFICER DURING THE SEPOY REVOLT *by A.R.D. Mackenzie*—Experiences with the 3rd Bengal Light Cavalry, the Guides and Sikh Irregular Cavalry from the outbreak to Delhi and Lucknow

THE ADVENTURES OF A LIGHT DRAGOON *by George Farmer & G.R. Gleig*—A cavalryman during the Peninsular & Waterloo Campaigns, in captivity & at the siege of Bhurtpore, India

THE COMPLEAT RIFLEMAN HARRIS *by Benjamin Harris as told to & transcribed by Captain Henry Curling*—The adventures of a soldier of the 95th (Rifles) during the Peninsular Campaign of the Napoleonic Wars

THE RED DRAGOON *by W.J. Adams*—With the 7th Dragoon Guards in the Cape of Good Hope against the Boers & the Kaffir tribes during the 'war of the axe' 1843-48

THE LIFE OF THE REAL BRIGADIER GERARD - Volume 1 - THE YOUNG HUSSAR 1782 - 1807 *by Jean-Baptiste De Marbot*—A French Cavalryman Of the Napoleonic Wars at Marengo, Austerlitz, Jena, Eylau & Friedland

THE LIFE OF THE REAL BRIGADIER GERARD Volume 2 IMPERIAL AIDE-DE-CAMP 1807 - 1811 *by Jean-Baptiste De Marbot*—A French Cavalryman of the Napoleonic Wars at Saragossa, Landshut, Eckmuhl, Ratisbon, Aspern-Essling, Wagram, Busaco & Torres Vedras

LEONAUR
CLASSIC SF FROM LEONAUR
AVAILABLE IN SOFTCOVER OR HARDCOVER WITH DUST JACKET

SF1 CLASSIC SCIENCE FICTION SERIES
BEFORE ADAM & Other Stories
by Jack London

Volume 1 of The Collected Science Fiction & Fantasy of Jack London.
SOFTCOVER : **ISBN 1-84677-008-4**
HARDCOVER : **ISBN 1-84677-015-7**

Contains the complete novel Before Adam plus shorter works: The Scarlet Plague, A Relic of the Pliocene, When the World Was Young, The Red One, Planchette, A Thousand Deaths, Goliah, A Curious Fragment and The Rejuvenation of Major Rathbone

SF2 CLASSIC SCIENCE FICTION SERIES
THE IRON HEEL & Other Stories
by Jack London

Volume 2 of The Collected Science Fiction & Fantasy of Jack London.
SOFTCOVER : **ISBN 1-84677-004-1**
HARDCOVER : **ISBN 1-84677-011-4**

Contains the complete novel The Iron Heel plus shorter works: The Enemy of All the World, The Shadow and the Flash, The Strength of the Strong, The Unparalleled Invasion and The Dream of Debs

SF3 CLASSIC SCIENCE FICTION SERIES
THE STAR ROVER & Other Stories
by Jack London

Volume 3 of The Collected Science Fiction & Fantasy of Jack London.
SOFTCOVER : **ISBN 1-84677-006-8**
HARDCOVER : **ISBN 1-84677-013-0**

Contains the complete novel The Star Rover plus shorter works: The Minions of Midas, The Eternity of Forms and The Man With the Gash